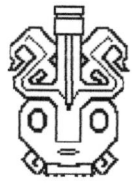

THE TRANSFORMATION OF NATURE IN ART

THE TRANSFORMATION OF NATURE IN ART

BY

ANANDA K. COOMARASWAMY

DOVER PUBLICATIONS

NEW YORK

Published in Canada by General Publishing Company, Ltd., 30 Lesmill Road, Don Mills, Toronto, Ontario.

Published in the United Kingdom by Constable and Company, Ltd., 10 Orange Street, London WC 2.

This Dover edition, first published in 1956, is an unabridged and unaltered republication of the second edition, as published by the Harvard University Press in 1934.

This edition is published by special arrangement with Harvard University Press.

International Standard Book Number: 0-486-20368-9

Manufactured in the United States of America
Dover Publications, Inc.
180 Varick Street
New York, N.Y. 10014

Contents

Chapter I

THE THEORY OF ART IN ASIA

Chapter I

THE THEORY OF ART IN ASIA

Tadbhavatu kṛtârthatā vaidagdhyasya,
Mālatīmādhava, I, 32 f.

IN THE following pages there is presented a statement of Oriental aesthetic theory based mainly on Indian and partly on Chinese sources; at the same time, by means of notes and occasional remarks, a basis is offered for a general theory of art coördinating Eastern and Western points of view. Whenever European art is referred to by way of contrast or elucidation, it should be remembered that "European art" is of two very different kinds, one Christian and scholastic, the other post-Renaissance and personal. It will be evident enough from our essay on Eckhart, and might have been made equally clear from a study of St Thomas and his sources, that there was a time when Europe and Asia could and did actually understand each other very well. Asia has remained herself; but subsequent to the extroversion of the European consciousness and its preoccupation with surfaces, it has become more and more difficult for European minds to think in terms of unity, and therefore more difficult to understand the Asiatic point of view. It is just possible that the mathematical development of modern science, and certain corresponding tendencies in modern European art on the one hand, and the penetration of Asiatic thought and art into the Western environment on the other, may represent the possibility of a renewed *rapprochement.* The peace and happiness of the world depend on this possibility. But for the present, Asiatic thought has hardly been, can hardly be, presented in European phraseology without distortion, and what is called the appreciation of Asiatic art is mainly based on categorical misinterpretations. Our purpose in the present volume is to place the Asiatic and the valid European views side by side, not as curiosities, but as representing actual and indispensable truth; not endeavoring to prove by any argumentation what should be apparent to the consciousness of the intelligent — *sacetasām anubhavaḥ pramāṇaṁ tatra kevalaṁ!*

The scope of the discussion permits only a brief reference to Muḥammadan art: Islāmic aesthetics could be presented only by an author steeped in Arabic philosophy and familiar with the literature on calligraphy, poetics, and the legitimacy of music. But it must be pointed out in passing that this Islāmic art, which in so many ways links East with West, and yet by its aniconic character seems to stand in opposition to both, really diverges not so much in fundamental principles as in literal interpretation. For naturalism is antipathetic to religious art of all kinds, to art of any kind, and the spirit of the traditional Islāmic interdiction of the representation of living forms is not really infringed by such ideal representations as are met with in Indian or Christian iconography, or Chinese animal painting. The Muḥammadan interdiction refers to such naturalistic representations as could theoretically, at the Judgment Day, be required to function biologically; but the Indian icon is not constructed as though to function biologically, the Christian icon cannot be thought of as moved by any other thing than its form, and each should, strictly speaking, be regarded as a kind of diagram, expressing certain ideas, and not as the likeness of anything on earth.

Let us now consider what is art and what are the values of art from an Asiatic, that is, mainly Indian and Far Eastern, point of view. It will be natural to lay most stress on India, because the systematic discussion of aesthetic problems has been far more developed there than in China, where we have to deduce the theory from what has been said and done by painters, rather than from any doctrine propounded by philosophers or rhetoricians.

In the first place, then, we find it clearly recognized that the formal element in art represents a purely mental activity, *citta-saññā*.[1] From this point of view, it will appear natural enough that India should have developed a highly specialized technique of vision. The maker of an icon, having by various means proper to the practice of Yoga eliminated the distracting influences of fugitive emotions and creature images, self-willing and self-thinking, proceeds to visualize the form of the *devatā*, angel or aspect of God, described in a given canonical prescription, *sādhana*, *mantram*, *dhyāna*. The mind "pro-duces" or "draws" (*ākarṣati*)[2] this form to itself, as though from a great distance. Ultimately, that is, from Heaven, where the types of art exist in formal operation; immediately, from "the immanent space in the heart" (*antar-hṛdaya-ākāśa*),[3] the common focus (*saṁstāva*, "concord")[4] of seer and seen, at which place the only possible experience of reality takes place.[5] The true-knowledge-purity-aspect (*jñāna-sattva-rūpa*) thus conceived and inwardly known (*antar-jñeya*) reveals itself against the ideal space (*ākāśa*) like a reflection (*pratibimbavat*), or as if seen in a dream (*svapnavat*). The imager must realize a complete self-identification with it (*ātmānaṁ . . . dhyāyāt*, or *bhāvayet*), whatever its peculiarities (*nānālakṣaṇâlaṁkṛtam*), even in the case of opposite sex or when the divinity is provided with terrible supernatural characteristics; the form thus known in an act of non-differentiation, being held in view as long as may be necessary (*evaṁ rūpaṁ yāvad icchati tāvad vibhāvayet*), is the model from which he proceeds to execution in stone, pigment, or other material.[6]

The whole process, up to the point of manufacture, belongs to the established order of personal devotions, in which worship is paid to an image mentally conceived (*dhyātvā yajet*); in any case, the principle involved is that true knowledge of an object is not obtained by merely empirical observation or reflex registration (*pratyakṣa*), but only when the knower and known, seer and seen, meet in an act transcending distinction (*anayor advaita*). To worship any Angel in truth one must become the Angel: "whoever worships a divinity as other than the self, thinking 'He is one, and I another,' knows not," *Bṛhadāraṇyaka Upaniṣad*, I, 4, 10.

The procedure on the part of the imager, above outlined, implies a real understanding of the psychology of aesthetic intuition. To generalize, whatever object may be the artist's chosen or appointed theme becomes for the time being the single object of his attention and devotion; and only when the theme has thus become for him an immediate experience can it be stated authoritatively from knowledge. Accordingly, the language of Yoga may be employed even in the case of a portrait, for example *Mālavikâgnimitra*, II, 2, where, the painter having missed something of the beauty of the model, this is attributed to a relaxation of concentration, an imperfect absorption, *śithila-samādhi*, not to want of observation. Even when a horse is to be modelled from life we still find the language of Yoga employed: "having concentrated, he should set to work" (*dhyātvā kuryāt*), *Śukranītisāra*, IV, 7, 73.

Here indeed European and Asiatic art meet on absolutely common ground; according to Eckhart, the skilled painter shows his art, but it is not himself that it reveals to us, and in the words of Dante, "Who paints a figure, if he cannot be it, cannot draw it," *Chi pinge figura, si non può esser lei, non la può porre.*[7] It should be added that the idea of Yoga covers not merely the moment of intuition, but also execution: Yoga is dexterity in action, *karmasu kauśala*, *Bhagavad Gītā*, II, 50. So, for example, in Śaṅkarâcārya's metaphor of the arrow-maker "who perceives nothing beyond his work when he is buried in it," and the saying, "I have learnt concentration from the maker of arrows." The words *yogyā*, application, study, practice, and *yukti*, accomplishment, skill, virtuosity, are often used in connection with the arts.

An ideal derivation of the types that are to be represented or made by the human artist is sometimes asserted in another way, all the arts being thought of as having a divine origin, and as having been revealed or otherwise brought down from Heaven to Earth: "our Śaiva Āgamas teach that the architecture of our temples is all Kailāsabhāvanā, that is of forms prevailing in Kailāsa." A very striking enunciation of this principle will be found in *Aitareya Brāhmaṇa*, VI, 27: "It is in imitation (*anukṛiti*) of the angelic (*deva*) works of art (*śilpāni*) that any work of art (*śilpa*) is accomplished (*adhigamyate*) here; for example, a clay elephant, a brazen object, a garment, a gold object, and a mule-chariot are 'works of art.' A work of art (*śilpa*), indeed (*ha*), is accomplished in him who comprehends this. For these (angelic) works of art (*śilpāni*, viz. the metrical Śilpa texts) are an integration of the Self (*ātma-saṁskṛti*); and by them the sacrificer likewise integrates himself (*ātmānaṁ saṁskurute*) in the mode of rhythm (*chandomaya*)." Corresponding to this are many passages of the *Ṛg Veda* in which the artistry of the incantation (*mantra*) is compared to that of a weaver or carpenter. Sometimes the artist is thought of as visiting some heaven, and there seeing the form of the angel or architecture to be reproduced on earth; sometimes the architect is spoken of as controlled by Viśvakarma, originally an essential name of the Supreme Artificer, later simply of the master architect of the angels, and patron of human craftsmen; or Viśvakarma may be thought of as himself assuming the form of a human architect in order to produce a particular work; or the required form may be revealed in a dream.[8]

Nor is any distinction of kind as between fine and decorative, free or servile, art to be made in this connection. Indian literature provides us with numerous lists of the eighteen or more professional arts (*śilpa*) and the sixty-four avocational arts (*kalā*); and these embrace every kind of skilled activity, from music, painting, and weaving to horsemanship, cookery, and the practice of magic, without distinction of rank, all being equally of angelic origin.[9]

It is thus, and will become further, evident that all the forms of Indian art and its derivatives in the Far East are ideally determined. We must now give greater precision to this statement, discussing what is implied in Asia by likeness or imitation, and what is the nature of Asiatic types. Lastly we shall be in a position to consider the formal theory of aesthetic experience.

First of all with regard to representation (*ākṛti*, *sādṛśya*, Ch. *hsing-ssŭ*, 4617, 10289, and *wu-hsing*, 12777, 4617) and imitation (*anukāra*, *anukaraṇa*, *anukṛti*). We find it stated that "*sādṛśya* is essential to the very substance (*pradhāna*) of painting," *Viṣṇudharmottara*, XLII, 48; the word has usually been translated by "likeness," and may bear this sense, but it will be shown below that the meaning properly implied is something more like "correspondence of formal and representative elements in art." In drama we meet with such definitions as *lokavṛtta-anukaraṇa*, "following the movement (or operation) of the world," and *yo 'yaṁ svabhāvo lokasya . . . nāṭyam ity abhidhīyate*,[10] "which designates the intrinsic nature of the world"; or again, what is to be exhibited on the stage is *avasthāna*, "conditions" or "emotional situations," or the hero, Rāma, or the like, is thought of as the model, *anukārya*.[11] In China, in the third canon of Hsieh Ho, we have "According to nature (*wu*, 12777) make shape (*hsing*, 4617)";[12] and the common later phrase *hsing-ssŭ*, "shape-resemblance," in the same way seems to define art as an imitation of Nature. In Japan, Seami, the great author and critic of Nō, asserts that the arts of music and dancing consist entirely in imitation (*monomane*).[13]

However, if we suppose that all this implies a conception of art as something seeking its perfection in the nearest possible approaches to illusion we shall be greatly mistaken. It will appear presently that we should err equally in supposing that Asiatic art represents an "ideal" world, a world "idealized" in the popular (sentimental, religious) sense of the words, that is, perfected or remolded nearer to the heart's desire; which were it so might be described as a blasphemy against the witness of Perfect Experience, and a cynical depreciation of life itself. We shall find that

Asiatic art is ideal in the mathematical sense: like Nature (*natura naturans*), not in appearance (viz. that of *ens naturata*), but in operation.

It should be realized that from the Indian (metaphysical) and Scholastic points of view, subjective and objective are not irreconcilable categories, one of which must be regarded as real to the exclusion of the other. Reality (*satya*) subsists there where the intelligible and sensible meet in the common unity of being, and cannot be thought of as existing in itself outside and apart from, but rather *as*, knowledge or vision, that is, only in act. All this is also implied in the Scholastic definition of truth as *adaequatio rei et intellectus*, Aristotle's identity of the soul with what it knows, or according to St Thomas, "knowledge comes about in so far as the object known is within the knower" (*Sum. Theol.*, I, Q. 59, A. 2), in radical contradiction to the conception of knowledge and being as independent acts, which point of view is only logically, and not immediately, valid. Translating this from psychological to theological terms, we should say not that God has knowledge, but that Knowledge (Pure Intellect, *prajñā*) is one of the names of God (who is pure act); or metaphysically, by an identification of Being (*sat*) with Intelligence (*cit*), as in the well-known concatenation *sac-cit-ānanda* (where it is similarly implied that love subsists only in the act of love, not in the lover or beloved but in union).

Now as to *sādṛśya*: literal meanings are sym-visibility, con-similarity; secondary meanings, coördination, analogy.

That aesthetic *sādṛśya* does not imply naturalism, verisimilitude, illustration, or illusion in any superficial sense is sufficiently shown by the fact that in Indian lists of factors essential to painting it is almost always mentioned with *pramāṇa*, "criterion of truth," here "ideal proportion"; in the Indian theories of knowledge empirical observation (*pratyakṣa*) as supplying only a test, and not the material of theory, is regarded as the least valid amongst the various *pramāṇas*. *Pramāṇa* will be discussed more fully below; here it will suffice to point out that the constant association of *sādṛśya* and *pramāṇa* in lists of the essentials in painting, for example the Six Limbs,[14] precludes our giving to either term a meaning flatly contradicting that of the other. Ideal form and natural shape, although distinct in principle, were not conceived as incommensurable, but rather as coincident in the common unity of the symbol.

In Rhetoric, *sādṛśya* is illustrated by the example "The young man is a lion" (Bhartṛmitra, *Abhidhā-vṛtti-mātrikā*, p. 17, and commonly quoted elsewhere); and this analogy very well demonstrates what is really meant by aesthetic "imitation." Vasubandhu, *Abhidharmakośa*, IX, Poussin, pp. 280, 281, explains the relation of knowledge (*vijñāna*) to its object by saying that knowledge arises only in the act of knowing, by an immediate assimilation (*tadākāratā*) to its object, neither knower nor known existing apart from the act of knowledge. The nature of the assimilation (*tadākāratā*) is illustrated by the *sādṛśya* of seed and fruit, which is one of reciprocal causality. The Nyāya-Vaiśeṣika definition of *sādṛśya* (quoted by Das Gupta, *History of Indian Philosophy*, I, 318) viz. *tadbhinnatve sati tadgata-bhūyodharmavattvam*, is literally "the condition of embracing in itself things of a manifold nature which are distinct from itself," or more briefly the condition of "identity in difference."

Sādṛśya is then "similitude," but rather such as is implied by "simile" than by "simulacrum." It is in fact obvious that the likeness between anything and any representation of it cannot be a likeness of nature, but must be analogical or exemplary, or both of these. What the representation imitates is the idea or species of the thing, by which it is known intellectually, rather than the substance of the thing as it is perceived by the senses.

Sādṛśya, "visual correspondence," has nevertheless been commonly misinterpreted as having to do with two appearances, that of the work of art and that of the model. It refers, actually, to a quality wholly self-contained within the work of art itself, a correspondence of mental and sensational factors in the work. This correspondence is indeed analogous to the correspondence of person and substance in the thing to be "imitated"; but the object and the work of art are independently determined, each to its own good, and physically incommensurable, being the same only as to type. *Sādṛśya* as the ground (*pradhāna*) of painting may be compared to *sāhitya* as the body (*śarīra*) of poetry, consistently defined as the "consent of sound and meaning" (*śabdârtha*), and to *sārūpya*, denoting the aspectual coördination of concept and percept essential to knowledge.[15] Accordingly, the requirement of *sādṛśya* does not merely not exclude the formal element in art, but positively asserts the necessity of a concord of pictorial and formal elements. The whole point of view outlined above is already implied in the *Kauṣītaki Upaniṣad*, III, 8, where the sensational and intelligible (formal) elements of appearance are distinguished as *bhūta-mātrā* and *prajñā-mātrā*, and it is asserted that "truly, from either alone, no aspect (*rūpa*) whatsoever would be produced."

As to the Indian drama, the theme is exhibited by means of gestures, speech, costume, and natural adaptation of the actor for the part; and of these four, the first three are highly conventional in any case, while with regard to the fourth not only is the appearance of the actor formally modified by make-up or even a mask, but Indian treatises constantly emphasize that the actor should not be carried away by the emotions he represents, but should rather be the ever-conscious master of the puppet show performed by his own body on the stage, The exhibition of his own emotions would not be art.[16]

As to Chinese *wu-hsing* and *hsing-ssŭ*, a multitude of passages could be adduced to show that it is not the outward appearance (*hsing*) as such, but rather the idea (*i*, 5367) in the mind of the artist, or the immanent divine spirit (*shên*, 9819), or the breath of life (*ch'i*, 1064), that is to be revealed by a right use of natural forms. We have not merely the first canon of Hsieh Ho, which asserts that the work of art must reveal "the operation (*yün*, 13817) of the spirit (*ch'i*) in life-movement," but also such sayings as "By means of natural shape (*hsing*) represent divine spirit (*shên*)," "The painters of old painted the idea (*i*) and not merely the shape (*hsing*)," "When Chao Tze Yün paints, though he makes few brush-strokes, he expresses the idea (*i*, 5367) already conceived; mere skill (*kung*, 6553) cannot accomplish (*nêng*) this" (*Ostasiatische Zeitschrift*, NF. 8, p. 105, text 4), or with reference to a degenerate period, "Those painters who neglect natural shape (*hsing*) and secure the formative idea (*i chih*, 5367, 1783) are few," "What the age means by pictures is resemblance (*ssŭ*)," and "The form was like (*hsing-ssŭ*), but the expression (*yün*, 13843) weak."

The Japanese Nō, which "can move the heart when not only representation but song, dance, mimic, and rapid action are all eliminated, emotion as it were springing out of quiescence," is actually the most formal and least naturalistic of all kinds of drama in the world.

Thus none of the terms cited by any means implies a view of art as finding its perfection in illusion; for the East, as for St Thomas, *ars imitatur naturam in sua operatione*.

The principle most emphasized in Indian treatises as essential to art is *pramāṇa*.[17] The Indian theories of knowledge regard as the source of truth not empirical perception (*pratyakṣa*) but an inwardly known model (*antarjñeya-rūpa*) "which at the same time gives form to knowledge and is the cause of knowledge" (Dignāga, *kārikā* 6), it being only required that such knowledge shall not contradict experience. It will be realized that this is also the method of science, which similarly uses experiment as the test rather than as the source of theory. *Pramāṇa* as principle is the self-evident immediate (*svataḥ*) perception of what is correct under given conditions. As independent of memory, *pramāṇa* cannot be identified with authority, but it may embody elements derived from authority, when considered not as principle but as canon. As not contrary to experience, *pramāṇa* means what is "true" here and now, but might not be correct in the light of wider experience or under changed conditions; in other words, the "development" of a theory is not excluded, nor the development of a design while in the course of execution. The doctrine can also be made clearer by the analogy of conscience, Anglo-Saxon "inwit," still understood as an inward criterion which at the same time gives form to conduct and is the cause of conduct. But whereas the Occidental conscience operates only in the field of ethics, and as to art a man is not ashamed to say "I know what I like," the Oriental conscience, *pramāṇa*, cf. Chinese *chih*, 1753, *liang*, 7015, *chêng*, 720 (used by Hsüan Tsang), *i*, 5367, etc., governs all forms of activity, mental, aesthetic, and ethical (*speculabilium, factibilium, agibilium*). Truth, Beauty, and Love as activities and therefore relative, are thus connected by analogy, and not by likeness, none deriving its sanction from any other, but each from a common principle of order inherent in the nature of God, or in Chinese terms of Heaven and Earth. To sum up, *pramāṇa* means in philosophy the norm of properly directed thought, in ethics the norm of properly directed action, in art the norm of properly conceived design, practically the *recta ratio factibilium* of St Thomas.

Thus the idea of *pramāṇa* implies the existence of types or archetypes, which might at first thought be compared with those of Plato and the derived European tradition. But whereas Platonic types are types of being, external to the conditioned universe and thought of as absolutes reflected in phenomena, Indian types are those of sentient activity or functional utility conceivable only in a contingent world. Oriental types, Indian Śiva-Śakti, Chinese Yang and Yin, or Heaven and Earth, are not thought of as mechanically reflected in phenomena, but as representing to our mentality the operative principles by which we "explain" phenomena — just as, for example, the concept of the shortest distance between two points may be said to "explain" the existence of a perceptible straight line. Thus Indian types representing sentiences or powers are analogous to those of Scholastic theology and the energies of science, but not comparable with Plato's types.

Just as conscience is externalized in rules of conduct, or the principles of thought in logic, so aesthetic *pramāṇa* finds expressions in rules (*vidhi*, *niyama*), or canons of proportion (*tāla*, *tālamāna*, *pramāṇāni*), proper to different types, and in the *lakṣaṇas* of iconography and cultivated taste, prescribed by authority and tradition; and only that art "which accords with canonical standards (*śāstra-māna*) is truly lovely, none other, forsooth!" (*Śukranītisāra*, IV, 4, 105–106). As to the necessity for such rules, contingent as they are by nature, and yet binding in a given environment, this follows from the imperfection of human nature as it is in itself. Man is indeed more than a merely instinctive and behavioristic animal, but he has not yet attained to such an identification of the inner and outer, contemplative and active, life as should enable him to act at the same time without discipline and altogether conveniently. On the one hand, the gambolling of lambs, however charming, is not yet dancing; on the other, the human artist, even the master whom Ching Hao calls "Profound" or "Mysterious" (*miao*, 7857) and who "works in a style appropriate to his subject," can hardly lay claim to the spontaneity of the "Divine" (*shên*, 9819) painter "who makes no effort of his own, his hand moves spontaneously."[18]

There exists, in fact, dating from the T'ang period, a threefold Chinese classification (*San p'ing*, 9552, 9273) of painting as Divine (*shên*, 9819), Profound or Mysterious (*miao*, 7857), and Accomplished (*nêng*, 8184). The first of these implies an absolute perfection; representing rather the goal than the attainable in human art; the second is such mastery as approaches perfection, the third is mere dexterity. A fourth class, the Marvellous or Extraordinary (*i*, 5536), was added later, with Taoist implications, to denote a more personal kind of "philosophical" or "literary" painting, great in achievement, though not the work of professional artists, and not governed by traditional rules; *i* thus corresponds very nearly to what is meant by "genius," with all its virtues and limitations.[19]

A striking Indian parallel to the *San p'ing* occurs in Rājaśekhara's *Kāvya-mīmāṁsā*, Ch. II, where the creative faculty (*kārayitrī pratibhā*) is considered as of three kinds, viz. Innate (*sahajā*), Gotten (*āhāryā*), and Learnt (*aupadeśikā*), poets being correspondingly classed as *sārasvata* (from Sarasvatī, Śakti of Brahmā, and mother of learning and wisdom), *ābhyāsika* (trained, adept, vocational), and *aupadeśika* (taught, depending on rules or recipes). Here *sārasvata* and *sahaja* clearly correspond to *shên*; *āhāryā* and *ābhyāsika* to *miao*, involving the idea of mastery; and *aupadeśikā* to *nêng*, having a trick rather than a habit. The one thing most necessary to the human workman is *abhyāsa*, "practice," otherwise thought of as *anuśīla*, "devoted application" or "obedience," the fruit of which is *śliṣṭatva*, "habitus," or second nature, skill, lit. "clingingness," "adherence"; and this finds expression in the performance as *mādhurya*, "grace" or "facility" (*Nāṭya Śāstra*, Benares ed., XXVI, 34; *Kāvyamālā* ed., XXII, 34).

The Six Canons of Hsieh Ho, referring to painting, were first published in the fifth century, and have remained authoritative to the present day. They have been discussed at great length by Far Eastern and European authors, the chief differences of opinion centering on the Taoist or Confucian interpretation of the first canon.[20] The following version is based directly on the text:

(1) Operation or revolution (*yün*, 13817), or concord or reverberation (*yün*, 13843), of the spirit (*ch'i*, 1064) in life movement.

(2) Rendering of the "bones" (essential structure) by the brush.

(3) According to the object (natural species, *wu*, 12777) make shape (*hsing*, 4617).

(4) According to the kind, apply, or distribute, color.

(5) Right composition, lit. "design due-placing."

(6) Traditional (*ch'uan*, 2740) procedure, lit. "handed down model, or method, draw accordingly."

Of these canons, the first is of primary metaphysical importance, and may be said to control all the others, each of which taken by itself has a straightforward meaning. The second canon demands a rendering of character rather than of mere outward aspect; the third and fourth refer to mass and color as means of representation; the fifth refers to the proper and appropriate placing of things represented, according to their natural relationships, and must thus be distinguished from composition or design in the sense in which these words are now used; the last implies the copying of ancient masterpieces and adherence to wonted methods and ascertained rules. These Six Canons have close analogies in Indian theory, but there is no good reason to suppose that they are of Indian origin.

In connection with the last canon, it may be remarked that a condition of spontaneity (*shên*, *sahaja*) outside of and above ascertained rules, though not against them, can be imagined, as in the *Bhagavad Gītā*, II, 46, where the knower of Brahman is said to have no further use for the Vedas, or when St Augustine says, "Love God, and do what you will." But if the liberated being (*jīvanmukta*) or saint in a state of grace is thus free to act without deliberation as to duty, it is because for him there no longer exists a separation of self and not-self; if for the true Yogin *pratyakṣa* must imply a presentation indistinguishable from that of the inwardly known form (*jñāna-sattva-rūpa*), this will be evidence, not of genius, but of a fully matured self (*kṛtâtman*), a perfected visual habit, such that the seer now sees not merely projected sensations, but as he ought to see, virtually without duality, loving all things alike.

All art thus tends towards a perfection in which pictorial and formal elements are not merely reconciled, but completely identified. At this distant but ever virtually present point, all necessity for art disappears, and the Islāmic doctors are justified in their assertion that the only true artist (*muṣavvir*) is God, in Indian terms *nirmāṇa-kāraka.*

The metaphor of God as the supreme artist appears also in the Christian Scholastic tradition, for example St Thomas, *Sum. Theol.*, Q. 74, A. 3, "as the giving form to a work of art is by means of the form of the art in the mind of the artist, which may be called his intelligible word, so the giving form to every creature is by the word of God; and for this reason in the works of distinction and adornment the Word is mentioned . . . the words, *God saw that it was good* . . . express a certain satisfaction taken by God in his works, as of an artist in his art." Eckhart makes constant use of the same idea. Cf. notes 21, 57. Needless to point out, the concept of "creation" (*nirmāṇa*, *karma*) is a religious (*bhaktivāda*) translation of what in metaphysics is spoken of as manifestation, procession, or expression (*sṛṣṭi*); or psychologically simply as a "coming to be" (*utpāda*, *bhava*, *yathā-bhūta*, etc.), dependent on second or mediate causes.

As the author of the *Chieh Tzŭ Yüan* expresses it, "When painting has reached divinity (*shên*) there is an end of the matter." A conception of this kind can be recognized in the Chinese story of the painter Wu Tao-tzŭ, who painted on a palace wall a glorious landscape, with mountains, forests, clouds, birds, men, and all things as in Nature, a veritable world-picture; while the Emperor his patron was admiring this painting, Wu Tao-tzŭ pointed to a doorway on the side of a mountain, inviting the Emperor to enter and behold the marvels within. Wu Tao-tzŭ himself entered first, beckoning the Emperor to follow; but the door closed, and the painter was never seen again. A corresponding disappearance of the work of art, when perfection has been attained, is mythically expressed in other legends, such as those of painted dragons that flew from the walls on which they were painted, first told of the artist Chang Sêng Yu in the Liang Dynasty.[21]

Such is the perfection toward which art and artist tend, art becoming manifested life, and the artist passing beyond our ken. But to lay claim therefore to a state of liberty and superiority to discipline (*anācāra*) on behalf of the human artist, to idolize one who is still a man as something more than man, to glorify rebellion and independence, as in the modern deification of genius and tolerance of the vagaries of genius, is plainly preposterous, or as Muslims would say blasphemous, for who shall presume to say that he indeed knows Brahman, or truly and completely loves God? The ultimate liberty of spontaneity is indeed conceivable only as a workless manifestation in which art and artist are perfected; but what thus lies beyond contingency is no longer "art," and in the meantime the way to liberty has nothing whatever in common with any wilful rebellion or calculated originality; least of all has it anything to do with functional self-expression. Ascertained rules should be thought of as the vehicle assumed by spontaneity, in so far as spontaneity is possible for us, rather than as any kind of bondage. Such rules are necessary to any being whose activity depends on will, as expressed in India with reference to the drama: "All the activities of the angels, whether at home in their own places, or abroad in the breaths of life, are intellectually emanated; those of men are put forth by conscious effort; therefore it is that the works to be done by men are defined in detail," *Nāṭya Śāstra*, II, 5. As expressed by St Thomas (*Sum. Theol.*, I, Q. 59, A. 2), "there alone are essence and will identified where all good is contained within the essence of him who wills . . . this cannot be said of any creature." In tending toward an ultimate coincidence of discipline and will, the artist does indeed become ever less and less conscious of rules, and for the virtuoso intuition and performance are already apparently simultaneous; but at every stage the artist will delight in rules, as the master of language delights in grammar, though he may speak without constant reference to the treatises on syntax. It is of the essence of art to bring back into order the multiplicity of Nature, and it is in this sense that he "prepares all creatures to return to God."

It should be hardly necessary to point out that art is by definition essentially conventional (*saṁketita*); for it is only by convention that nature can be made intelligible, and only by signs and symbols, *rūpa*, *pratīka*, that communication is made possible. A good example of the way in which we take the conventionality of art for granted is afforded by the story of a famous master who was commissioned to paint a bamboo forest. With magnificent skill he painted entirely in red. The patron objected that this was unnatural. The painter enquired, "In what color should it have been painted?" and the patron replied, "In black, of course." "And who," said the artist, "ever saw a black-leaved bamboo?" [22]

The whole problem of symbolism (*pratīka*, "symbol") is discussed by Śaṅkarâcārya, Commentary on the *Vedânta Sūtras*, I, 1, 20. Endorsing the statement that "all who sing here to the harp, sing Him," he points out that this Him refers to the highest Lord only, who is the ultimate theme even of worldly songs. And as to anthropomorphic expressions in scripture, "we reply that the highest Lord may, when he pleases, assume a bodily shape formed of Māyā, in order to gratify his devout worshippers"; but all this is merely analogical, as when we say that the Brahman abides here or there, which in reality abides only in its own glory (cf. *ibid.*, I, 2, 29). The representation of the invisible by the visible is also discussed by Deussen, *Philosophy of the Upanishads*, pp. 99–101. For a discussion of "sign" and "symbol" see pp. 125–127.

Conventionality has nothing to do with calculated simplification (as in modern designing), or with degeneration from representation (as often assumed by the historians of art). It is unfortunate indeed that the word conventional should have come to be used in a deprecatory sense with reference to decadent art. Decadent art is simply an art which is no longer felt or energized, but merely denotes, in which there exists no longer any real correspondence between the formal and pictorial elements, its meaning as it were negated by the weakness or incongruity of the pictorial element; but it is often, as for example in late Hellenistic art, actually *far less* conventional than are the primitive or classic stages of the same sequence. True art, pure art, never enters into competition with the unattainable perfection of the world, but relies exclusively on its own logic and its own criteria, which cannot be tested by standards of truth or goodness applicable in other fields of activity. If, for example, an icon is provided with numerous heads or arms, or combines anthropomorphic and theriomorphic elements, arithmetic and observation will assist us to determine whether or not the iconography is correct (*āgamârthâvisaṁvādi, śāstramāna*), but only our own response to its qualities of energy and characteristic order will enable us to judge it as a work of art. If Kṛṣṇa is depicted as the seducer of the milkmaids of Braja, it would be ridiculous to raise objections on moral grounds, as though a model on the plane of conduct had been presented; for here art, by a well understood convention, deals with the natural relation of the soul to God ("all creation is female to God"), and if we cannot understand or will not accept the tradition, that is simply an announcement of our inability to pass aesthetic judgment in the given case.

Some further considerations upon unequal quality and decadence in art may be submitted, by decadence "characteristic imperfection" being meant rather than the opposite of "progress." Any lack of temporal perfection in a work of art is a betrayal of the imperfection of the artist, such perfection as is possible to human work being a product of the will. It is obvious that the workman's first consideration should have been the good of the work to be done, for it is only so that he can praise his theme; and as to whether the work is in this sense good, we ought to be guided by a proper and ruthless critical faculty. But it should not be overlooked that even in outwardly imperfect works, whether originally so or having become so through damage, the image may remain intact; for in the first case the image, which was not of the artist's own invention but inherited, can still be recognized in its imperfect embodiment, and in the second the form by which the art was moved must have been immanent in every part of it, and is thus present in what survives of it, and this is why such works may be adequate to evoke in a strong-minded spectator a true aesthetic experience, such a one supplying by his own imaginative energy all that is lacking in the original production. More often, of course, what passes for an appreciation of decadent or damaged work is merely a sentimental pleasure based on associated ideas, *vāsanā qua* nostalgia.

There are two distinguishable modes of decadence in art, one corresponding to a diminished sensuality, the other reflecting, not an animal attachment to sensation, but a senescent refinement. It is essential to distinguish this attenuation or over-refinement of what was once a classical art from the austerity of primitive forms which may be less seductive, but express a high degree of intellectuality. Over-refinement and elaboration of apparatus in the arts are well illustrated in modern dramatic and concert production, and in the quality of trained voices and instruments such as the piano. All these means at the disposal of the artist are the means of his undoing, except in the rare cases where he can still by a real devotion to his theme make us forget them. Those accustomed to such comfortable arts as these are in real danger of rejecting less highly finished or less elaborate products, not at all on aesthetic grounds, but out of pure laziness and love of comfort. One thinks by contrast of the Bengālī *Yātrās* that "without scenery, without the artistic display of costumes, could rouse emotions which nowadays we scarcely experience," or, on the other hand, of utterly sophisticated arts like the Nō plays of Japan, in which the means have been reduced to a minimum, and though they have been brought to that high pitch of perfection that the theme demands, are yet entirely devoid of any element of luxury. These points of view have been discussed by Rabindranath Tagore in connection with the rendition of Indian music. "Our master singers," he says, "never take the least trouble to make their voice and manner attractive. . . . Those of the audience . . . whose senses have to be satisfied as well are held to be beneath the notice of any self-respecting artist," while "those of the audience who are appreciative are content to perfect the song in their own mind by the force of their own feeling." In other words, while the formal beauty is the essential in art, loveliness and convenience are, not indeed fortuitous, but in the proper sense of the word, accidents of art, happy or unhappy accidents as the case may be.

We are now in a position to describe the peculiarities of Oriental art with greater precision. The Indian or Far Eastern icon, carved or painted, is neither a memory image nor an idealization, but a visual symbolism, ideal in the mathematical sense. The "anthropomorphic" icon is of of the same kind as a *yantra*, that is, a geometrical representation of a deity, or a *mantra*, that is, an auditory representation of a deity. The peculiarity of the icon depends immediately upon these conditions, and could not be otherwise explained, even were we unaware that in actual practice it *is* the *mantra* and not the eye's intrinsic faculty that originates the image. Accordingly, the Indian icon fills the whole field of vision at once, all is equally clear and equally essential; the eye is not led to range from one point to another, as in empirical vision, nor to seek a concentration of meaning in one part more than in another, as in a more "theatrical" art. There is no feeling of texture or flesh, but only of stone, metal, or pigment, the object being an image in one or other of these materials, and not a deceptive replica (*savarṇa*) of any objective cause of sensation. The parts of the icon are not organically related, for it is not contemplated that they should function biologically, but ideally related, being the required component parts of a given type of activity stated in terms of the visible and tangible medium. This does not mean that the various parts are not related, or that the whole is not a unity, but that the relation is mental rather than functional. These principles will apply as much to landscape as to iconography.

In Western art the picture is generally conceived as seen in a frame or through a window, and so brought toward the spectator; but the Oriental image really exists only in our own mind and heart and is thence projected or reflected onto space. The Western presentation is designed as if seen from a fixed point of view, and must be optically plausible; Chinese landscape is typically represented as seen from more than one point of view, or in any case from a conventional, not a "real," point of view, and here it is not plausibility but intelligibility that is essential. In painting generally there is relievo (*natônnata*, *nimnônnata*), that is to say modelling in abstract light, painting being thought of as a constricted *mode* of sculpture; but never before the European influence in the seventeenth century any use of cast shadows, chiaroscuro, *chāyâtapa*, "shade and shine." Methods of representing space in art will always correspond more or less to contemporary habits of vision, and nothing more than this is required for art; perspective is nothing but the means employed to convey to the spectator the idea of three-dimensional space, and among the different kinds of perspective that have been made use of, the one called "scientific" has no particular advantage from the aesthetic point of view. On this point, Asaṅga, *Mahāyāna Sūtrâlaṁkāra*, XIII, 17, is illuminating: *citre . . . natônnataṁ nâsti ca, dṛśyate atha ca*, "there is no actual relief in a painting, and yet we see it there," an observation which is repeated from the same point of view in the *Laṅkâvatāra Sūtra*, Nanjio's ed., p. 91.[23] It would be thus as much beside the mark to conceive of a progress in art as revealed by a development in *Raumdarstellung* as to seek to establish a stylistic sequence on a supposed more or less close observation of Nature. Let us not forget that the mind is a part, and the most important part, of our knowledge of Nature, and that this point of view, though it may have been forgotten in Europe, has been continuously current in Asia for more than two thousand years.

Where European art naturally depicts a moment of time,

an arrested action or an effect of light, Oriental art represents a continuous condition. In traditional European terms, we should express this by saying that modern European art endeavors to represent things as they are in themselves, Asiatic and Christian art to represent things more nearly as they are in God, or nearer to their source. As to what is meant by representing a continuous condition, for example, the Buddha attained Enlightenment countless ages since, his manifestation is still accessible, and will so remain; the Dance of Śiva takes place, not merely in the Tāraka forest, nor even at Cidambaram, but in the heart of the worshipper; the Kṛṣṇa Līlā is not an historical event, of which Nīlakaṇṭha reminds us, but, using Christian phraseology, a "play played eternally before all creatures." This point of view, which was by no means unknown to the European schoolmen and is still reflected in India's so-called lack of any historical sense, Islam and China being here nearer to the world than India, though not so enmeshed in the world as modern Europe, constitutes the *a priori* explanation of the Indian adherence to types and indifference to transient effects. One might say, not that transient effects are meaningless, but that their value is not realized except to the degree that they are seen *sub specie aeternitatis*, that is *formaliter*. And where it is not the event but the type of activity that constitutes the theme, how could the East have been interested in cast shadows? Or how could the Śūnyavādin, who may deny that any Buddha ever really existed, or that any doctrine was ever actually taught, and so must be entirely indifferent as to the historicity of the Buddha's life, have been curious about the portraiture of Buddha? It would indeed be irrelevant to demand from any art a solution of problems of representation altogether remote from contemporary interest.

Little as it might have been foreseen, the concept of types prevails also in the portraiture of individuals, where the model is present (*pratyakṣa*) to the eye or memory. It is true that classical Indian portraits must have been recognizable, and even admirable, likenesses. We have already seen that *sādṛśya*, conformity of sense and substance, is essential in painting, and it has been pointed out that different, though closely related, terms, viz. *sadṛśī* and *susadṛśī*, are employed when the idea of an exact or speaking likeness is to be expressed.[24] The painted portrait (*pratikṛti*, *ākṛti*) functioned primarily as a substitute for the living presence of the original. One of the oldest treatises, the Tanjur *Citralakṣaṇa*, refers the origin of painting in the world to this requirement, and yet actually treats only the physiognomical peculiarities (*lakṣaṇa*) of types. Even more instructive is a later case, occurring in one of the *Vikramacaritra* stories: here the King is so much attached to the Queen that he keeps her at his side, even in council, but this departure from custom and propriety is disapproved of by the courtiers, and the King consents to have a portrait painted, as a substitute for the Queen's presence. The court painter is allowed to see the Queen; he recognizes that she is a *padminī*, that is, a "Lotus-lady," one of the four types under which women are classed according to physiognomy and character by Hindu rhetoricians. He paints her accordingly *padminī-lakṣaṇa-yuktam*, "with the characteristic marks of a Lotus-lady," and yet the portrait is spoken of not merely as *rūpam*, a figure, but even as *svarūpam*, "her intrinsic aspect." We know also, both in China and in India, of ancestral portraits, but these were usually prepared after death, and so far as preserved have the character of effigies (Chinese *ying-tu*, "diagram of a shade") rather than of speaking likenesses. In the *Pratimā-nāṭaka*, the hero, marvelling at the execution of the statues in an ancestral chapel, does not recognize them as those of his parents, and wonders if they are representations of deities. We even find a polemic against portraiture: "images of the angels are productive of good, and heaven-ward-leading, but those of men or other mortal beings lead not to heaven nor work weal," *Śukranītisāra*, IV, 4, 75 and 76. Chinese ancestral portraits are not devoid of individual characterization, but this represents only a slight, not an essential, modification of general formulae; the books on portraiture (*fu shên*, "depicting soul") refer only to types of features, canons of proportion, suitable accessories, and varieties of brush stroke proper for the draperies; the essence of the subject must be portrayed, but there is nothing said about anatomical accuracy. The painter Kuo Kung-ch'ên was praised for his rendering of very soul (*ching shên*, 2133, 9819) and mind (*i ch'u*, 5367, 3120) in a portrait; but there cannot be adduced from the whole of

Asia such a thing as a treatise on anatomy designed for use by artists.

The first effect produced on a modern Western spectator by these scholastic qualities of Oriental art is one of monotony. In literature and plastic art, persons are not so much distinguished as individuals as by what they do, in which connection it may be remembered that orthodoxy, for the East, is determined by what a man does, and not by his beliefs. Again, the productions of any one period are characterized far more by what is common to them all than by the personal variations. Because of their exclusively professional character and formal control, and the total absence of the conception of private property in ideas, the range of quality and theme that can be found in Oriental works of one and the same age or school is less than that which can be seen in European art at the present day, and besides this, identical themes and formulae have been adhered to during long periods. Where the modern student, accustomed to an infinite variety of choice in themes, and an infinite variety and tolerance of personal mannerisms, has neither accustomed himself to the idea of an unanimous style, nor to that of themes determined by general necessities and unanimous demand, nor learned to distinguish nuances in the unfamiliar stylistic sequences, his impatience can hardly be wondered at; but this impatience, which is not a virtue, must be outgrown. Here is involved the whole question of the distinction between originality or novelty and intensity or energy; it should be enough to say that when there is realization, when the themes are felt and art *lives*, it is of no moment whether or not the themes are new or old.

Life itself—the different ways in which the difficult problems of human association have been solved—represents the ultimate and chief of the arts of Asia; and it must be stated once for all that the forms assumed by this life are by no means empirically determined, but designed as far as possible according to a metaphysical tradition, on the one hand conformably to a divine order, and on the other with a view to facilitating the attainment by each individual of approximate perfection in his kind, that is, permitting him, by an exact adjustment of opportunity to potentiality, to achieve such realization of his entire being as is possible to him. Even town-planning depends in the last analysis upon considerations of this kind. Neither the society nor the specific arts can be rationally enjoyed without a recognition of the metaphysical principles to which they are thus related, for things can be enjoyed only in proportion to their intelligibility, speaking, that is, humanly and not merely functionally.

Oriental life is modelled on types of conduct sanctioned by tradition. For India, Rāma and Sītā represent ideals still potent, the *svadharma* of each caste is a *mode* of behavior, good form being *à la mode*; and until recently every Chinese accepted as a matter of course the concept of manners established by Confucius. The Japanese word for rudeness means "acting in an unexpected way." Here, then, life is designed like a garden, not allowed to run wild. All this formality, for a cultured spectator, is far more attractive than can be the variety of imperfection so freely displayed by the plain and blunt, or as he thinks, "more sincere," European. This external conformity, whereby a man is lost in the crowd as true architecture seems to be a part of its native landscape, constitutes for the Oriental himself a privacy within which the individual character can flower unhampered. This is most of all true in the case of women, whom the East has so long sheltered from necessities of self-assertion; one may say that for women of the aristocratic classes in India or Japan there has existed no freedom whatever in the modern sense, yet these same women, molded by centuries of stylistic living, achieved an absolute perfection in their kind, and perhaps Asiatic art can show no higher achievement than this. In India, where the "tyranny of caste" strictly governs marriage, diet, and every detail of outward conduct, there exists and has always existed unrestricted freedom of thought as to modes of belief or thought; a breach of social etiquette may involve excommunication from society, but religious intolerance is practically unknown, and it is a perfectly normal thing for different members of the same family to choose for themselves the particular deity of their personal devotion.

It has been well said that civilization is style. An immanent culture in this sense endows every individual with an outward grace, a typological perfection, such as only the rarest beings can achieve by their own effort, a kind of perfection which does not belong to genius; whereas a democracy, which requires of every man to save his own "face" and soul, actually condemns each to an exhibition of his own irregularity and imperfection, and this implicit acceptance of formal imperfection only too easily passes over into an exhibitionism which makes a virtue of vanity and is complacently described as self-expression.

We have so far discussed the art of Asia in its theological aspect, that is with reference to the scholastic organization of thought in terms of types of activity, and the corresponding arts of symbolism and iconography, in which the elements of form presented by Nature and redeemed by art are used as means of communication. The classical developments of this kind of art belong mainly to the first millennium of the Christian era. Its later prolongations tend to decadence, the formal elements retaining their edifying value, in design and composition, but losing their vitality, or surviving only in folk art, where the intensity of an earlier time expressing a more conscious will is replaced by a simpler harmony of style prevailing throughout the whole man-made environment. Eighteenth-century Siam and Ceylon provide us with admirable examples of such a folk style based on classical tradition, this condition representing the antithesis of that now realized in the West, where in place of vocation as the general type of activity we find the types of individual genius on the one hand, and that of unskilled labor on the other.

Another kind of art, sometimes called romantic or idealistic, but better described as imagist [25] or mystical, where denotation and connotation cannot be divided, is typically developed throughout Asia in the second millennium. In this kind of art no distinction is felt between what a thing "is" and what it "signifies." However, in thus drawing a distinction between symbolic and imagist art it must be very strongly emphasized that the two kinds of art are inseverably connected and related historically and aesthetically; for example, Kamakura Buddhist painting in the twelfth or thirteenth century is still iconographic, in Sung landscape and animal painting there is always an underlying symbolism, and, on the other hand, Indian animal sculpture at Māmallapuram in the seventh century is already romantic, humorous, and mystical. A more definite break between the two points of view is illustrated in the well-known story of the Zen priest Tan-hsia, who used a wooden image of the Buddha to make his fire — not however, as iconoclast, but simply because he was cold. The two kinds of art are most closely connected by the philosophy and practice of Yoga; in other words, a self-identification with the theme is always prerequisite. But whereas the theological art is concerned with types of power, the mystical art is concerned with only one power. Its ultimate theme is that single and undivided principle which reveals itself in every form of life whenever the light of the mind so shines on anything that the secret of its inner life is realized, both as an end in itself unrelated to any human purpose, and as no other than the secret of one's own innermost being. "When thou seest an eagle, thou seest a portion of genius"; "the heavens declare the glory of God"; "a mouse is miracle enough," these are European analogies; or St Bernard's *Ligna et lapides docebunt te, quod a magistris audire non posse.*

Here, then, the proximate theme may be any aspect of Nature whatsoever, not excluding human nature but "wherever the mind attaches itself," every aspect of life having an equal value in a spiritual view. In theory this point of view could be applied in justification of the greatest possible variety of individual choice, and interpreted as a "liberation" of the artist from associated ideas. However, in the more practical economy of the great living traditions we find, as before, that certain restricted kinds or groups of themes are adhered to generation after generation in a given area, and that the technique is still controlled by most elaborate rules, and can only be acquired in long years of patient practice (*abhyāsa*). Historical conditions and environment, an inheritance of older symbolisms, specific racial sensibilities, all these provide a better than private determination of the work to be done; for the artist or artisan, who "has his art which he is expected to practice," this is a means to the conservation of energy; for man generally, it secures a continued comprehensibility of art, its value as communication.

The outstanding aspects of the imagist or mystical art of Asia are the Ch'an or Zen [26] art of China and Japan, in which the theme is either landscape or plant or animal life;

Vaiṣṇava painting, poetry, and music in India, where the theme is sexual love; and Ṣūfī poetry and music in Persia, devoted to the praise of intoxication.

The nature of Ch'an Zen is not easy to explain. Its sources are partly Indian, partly Taoist, its development both Chinese and Japanese. Chinese Buddhist art is *like* Indian in general aspect, differing only in style; Ch'an-Zen art provides us with a perfect example of that kind of real assimilation of new cultural ideas which results in a development formally *unlike* the original. This is altogether different from that hybridization which results from "influences" exerted by one art upon another; influences in this last sense, though historians of art attach great importance to them, are almost always manifested in unconscious parody, — one thinks of Hellenistic art in India, or *chinoiseries* in Europe, — and in any case belong to the history of taste rather than to the history of art. At the same time that we recognize Indian sources of Ch'an-Zen art, it is to be remembered that Zen is also deeply rooted in Taoism; it is sufficiently shown by the saying of Chuang Tzŭ, "The mind of the sage, being in repose, becomes the mirror of the universe, the speculum of all creation," that China had always and independently been aware of the true nature of imaginative vision.

The Ch'an-Zen discipline is one of activity and order; its doctrine the invalidity of doctrine, its end an illumination by immediate experience. Ch'an-Zen art, seeking realization of the divine being in man, proceeds by way of opening his eyes to a like spiritual essence in the world of Nature external to himself; the scripture of Zen "is written with the characters of heaven, of man, of beasts, of demons, of hundreds of blades of grass, and of thousands of trees" (Dōgen), "every flower exhibits the image of Buddha" (Dugō). A good idea of Ch'en-Zen art can be obtained from the words of a twelfth-century Chinese critic, writing on animal painting: after alluding to the horse and bull as symbols of Heaven and Earth, he continues: "But tigers, leopards, deer, wild swine, fawns, and hares — creatures that cannot be inured to the will of man — these the painter chooses for the sake of their skittish gambols and swift shy evasions, loves them as things that seek the desolation of great plains and wintry snows, as creatures that will not be haltered with a bridle, nor tethered by the foot. He would commit to brushwork the gallant splendor of their stride; *this he would do and no more.*" [27] But the Ch'an-Zen artist no more paints from Nature than the poet writes from Nature; he has been trained according to treatises on style so detailed and explicit that there would seem to be no room left for the operation of personality. A Japanese painter once said to me, "I have had to concentrate on the bamboo for many, many years, still a certain technique for the rendering of the tips of bamboo leaves eludes me." And yet immediacy or spontaneity has been more nearly perfectly attained in Ch'an-Zen art than anywhere else. Here there is no formal iconography, but an intuition that has to be expressed in an ink painting where no least stroke of the brush can be erased or modified; the work is as irrevocable as life itself. There is no kind of art that comes nearer to "grasping the joy as it flies," the winged life that is no longer life when we have taken thought to remember and describe it; no kind of art more studied in method, or less labored in effect. Every work of Ch'an-Zen art is unique, and in proportion to its perfection inscrutable.

But Ch'an-Zen is by no means only a way to perfect experience, it is also a way to the perfecting of character. Ch'an-Zen represents all and more than we now mean by the word "culture": an active principle pervading every aspect of human life, becoming now the chivalry of the warrior, now the grace of the lover, now the habit of the craftsman. The latter point may be illustrated by Chuang Tzŭ's story of the wheelwright who ventured to criticize a nobleman for reading the works of a dead sage. In excusing his temerity, he explained: "Your humble servant must regard the matter from the point of view of his own art. In making a wheel, if I proceed too gently, that is easy enough, but the work will not stand fast; if I proceed too violently, that is not only toilsome, but the parts will not fit well together. It is only when the movements of my hand are neither too gentle nor too violent that the idea in my mind can be realized. Still, I cannot explain this in words; there is a skill in it which I cannot teach my son, nor can he learn it from me." The wheelwright pointed out, in other words, that perfection cannot be achieved by reading about it, but only in direct action.

Thus Ch'an-Zen is by no means an asceticism divorced from life, though there are many great Ch'an-Zen monasteries; Ch'an-Zen art presents no exception to the general rule in Asia, that all works of art have definite and commonly understood meanings, apart from any aesthetic perfection of the work itself. The meanings of Ch'an-Zen themes are such as have sometimes been expressed in European art by means of allegorical figures. Dragon and tiger, mist and mountain, horse and bull, are types of Heaven and Earth, spirit and matter; the gentle long-armed gibbon suggests benevolence, the peacock is symbolic of longevity, the lotus represents an immaculate purity. Let us consider the case of the pine tree and the morning glory, both favorite themes of Japanese art: "The morning glory blossoms only for an hour, and yet it differs not at heart from the pine, which may endure for a thousand years." What is to be understood here is not an obvious allegory of time and eternity, but that the pine no more takes thought of its thousand years than the morning glory of its passing hour; each fulfils its destiny and is content; and Matsunaga, the author of the poem, wished that his heart might be like theirs. If such associations add nothing directly to aesthetic quality, neither do they in any way detract from it. When at last Zen art found expression in scepticism,

Granted this dewdrop world is but a dewdrop world,
This granted, yet . . . [28]

there came into being the despised popular and secular

Ukiyoye[29] art of Japan. But here an artistic tradition had been so firmly established, the vision of the world so *approfondi*, that in a sphere corresponding with that of the modern picture postcard — Ukiyoye illustrated the theatre, the *Yoshiwara*, and the *Aussichtspunkt* — there still survived a purity and charm of conception that sufficed, however slight their essence, to win acceptance in Europe, long before the existence of a more serious and classical art had been suspected.

A mystical development took place in India somewhat later, and on different lines. In the anthropocentric European view of life, the nude human form has always seemed to be peculiarly significant, but in Asia, where human life has been thought of as differing from that of other creatures, or even from that of the "inanimate" creation only in degree, not in kind, this has never been the case. On the other hand, in India, the conditions of human love, from the first meeting of eyes to ultimate self-oblivion, have seemed spiritually significant, and there has always been a free and direct use of sexual imagery in religious symbolism. On the one hand, physical union has seemed to present a self-evident image of spiritual unity; on the other, operative forces, as in modern scientific method, are conceived as male and female, positive and negative. It was thus natural enough that later Vaiṣṇava mysticism, speaking always of devotion, *bhakti*, should do so in the same terms; the true and timeless relation of the soul to God could now only be expressed in impassioned epithalamia celebrating the nuptials of Rādhā and Kṛṣṇa, milkmaid and herdsman, earthly Bride and heavenly Bridegroom. So there came into being songs and dances in which at one and the same time sensuality has spiritual significance, and spirituality physical substance, and painting that depicts a transfigured world, where all men are heroic, all women beautiful and passionate and shy, beasts and even trees and rivers are aware of the presence of the Beloved — a world of imagination and reality, seen with the eyes of Majñūn.[30] If in the dance ("nautch") the mutual relations of hero and heroine imitated by the players display an esoteric meaning,[31] this is not by arbitrary interpretation or as allegory, but by a mutual introsusception. If in painting and poetry the daily life of peasants seemed to reflect conditions ever present in the pastoral Heaven of the Divine Cowherd, this is not a sentimental or romantic symbolism, but born of the conviction that "all the men and women of the world are His living forms" (Kabīr), that reality is here and now tangibly and visibly accessible. Here the scent of the earth is ever present: "If he has no eyes, nor nose, nor mouth, how could he have stolen and eaten curd? Can we abandon our love of Kṛṣṇa, to worship a figure painted on a wall?" (Sūr Dās.) Realities of experience, and neither a theory of design nor inspiration coming none knows whence, are the sources of this art; and those who cannot at least in fancy (*vāsanā*)[32] experience the same emotions and sense their natural operation cannot expect to be able to understand the art by any other and more analytical processes. For no art can be judged until we place ourselves at the point of view of the artist; so only can the determination be known by which its design and execution are entirely controlled.

A formal theory of art based on the facts as above outlined has been enunciated in India in a considerable literature on Rhetoric (*alaṁkāra*). It is true that this theory is mainly developed in connection with poetry, drama, dancing, and music, but it is immediately applicable to art of all kinds, much of its terminology employs the concept of color, and we have evidence that the theory was also in fact applied to painting.[33] Accordingly, in what follows we have not hesitated to give an extended interpretation to terms primarily employed in connection with poetry, or rather literature (*kāvya*), considered as the type of art.[34] The justification of art is then made with reference to use (*prayojana*) or value (*puruṣârtha*)[35] by pointing out that it subserves the Four Purposes of Life, viz. Right Action (*dharma*), Pleasure (*kāma*), Wealth (*artha*), and Spiritual Freedom (*mokṣa*). Of these, the first three represent the proximate, the last the ultimate, ends of life; the work of art is determined (*prativihita*) in the same way, proximately with regard to immediate use, and ultimately with regard to aesthetic experience. Art is then defined as follows: VAKYAṀ RASÂTMAKAṀ KĀVYAM, that is, "ART IS EXPRESSION INFORMED BY IDEAL BEAUTY."[36] Mere narration (*nirvāha*, *itihāsa*), bare utility, are not art, or are only art in a rudimentary sense. Nor has art as such a merely informative value confined to its explicit meaning (*vyutpatti*): only the man of little wit (*alpabuddhi*) can fail to recognize that art is by nature a well-spring of delight (*ānanda-niṣyanda*), whatever may have been the occasion of its appearance.[37] On the other hand, there cannot be imagined an art without meaning or use. The doctrine of art for art's sake is disposed of in a sentence quoted in the *Sāhitya Darpaṇa* V, 1, Commentary: "All expressions (*vākya*), human or revealed, are directed to an end beyond themselves (*kārya-param*, 'another *factibile*'); or if not so determined (*atatparatve*) are thereby comparable only to the utterances of a madman." Therefore, "let the purpose (*kṛtârthatā*) of skill (*vaidagdhya*) be attained," *Mālatīmādhava*, I, 32 f. Again, the distinction of art (controlled workmanship, things well and truly made) from Nature (functional expression, *sattva-bhāva*) is made as follows: "the work (*karma*) of the two hands is an otherwise-determined (*parastāt-prativihitā*) element of natural being (*bhūta-mātrā*)," *Kauṣītaki Upaniṣad*, III, 5.

In this theory of art, the most important term is RASA, rendered above "Ideal Beauty," but meaning literally "tincture" or essence, and generally translated in the present connection as "flavor"; aesthetic experience being described as the tasting of flavor (*rasâsvādana*) or simply as tasting (*svāda, āsvāda*), the taster as *rasika*, the work of art as *rasavat*.[38] It should also be observed that the word *rasa* is used (1) relatively, in the plural, with reference to the various, usually eight or nine, emotional conditions which may constitute the burden of a given work, love (*śṛṅgāra-rasa*) being the most significant of these, and (2) absolutely, in the singular, with reference to the interior act of tasting flavor unparticularized. In the latter sense, which alone need be considered here, the idea of an aesthetic beauty to be tast*ed*, and knowable only in the activity of tast*ing*,[39] is to be clearly distinguished from the relative beauties or lovelinesses of the separate parts of the work, or of the work itself considered merely as a surface, the appreciation of all which is a matter of taste (*ruci*) or predilection.[40] The latter relative beauties will appear in the theme and aesthetic surfaces, in all that has to do with the proximate determination of the work to be done, its ordering to use; the formal beauty will be sensed in vitality and unity, design and rhythm, in no way depending on the nature of the theme, or its component parts. It is indeed very explicitly pointed out that any theme whatever, "lovely or unlovely, noble or vulgar, gracious or frightful, etc.," may become the vehicle of *rasa*.[41]

The definition of aesthetic experience (*rasâsvādana*) given in the *Sāhitya Darpaṇa*, III, 2–3, is of such authority and value as to demand translation *in extenso*; we offer first, a very literal version with brief comment, then a slightly smoother rendering avoiding interruptions. Thus, (1) "Flavor (*rasaḥ*) is tasted (*āsvādyate*) by men having an innate knowledge of absolute values (*kaiścit-pramātṛbhiḥ*), in exaltation of the pure consciousness (*sattvôdrekāt*), as self-luminous (*svaprakāśaḥ*), in the mode at once of ecstasy and intellect (*ānanda-cin-mayaḥ*), void of contact with things knowable (*vedyântara-sparśa-śūnyaḥ*), twin brother to the tasting of Brahma (*brahmâsvāda-sahôdaraḥ*), whereof the life is a super-wordly lightning-flash (*lokôttara-camatkāra-prâṇaḥ*), as intrinsic aspect (*svâkāravat = svarūpavat*), in indivisibility (*abhinnatve*)": and (2) "Pure aesthetic experience is theirs in whom the knowledge of ideal beauty is innate; it is known intuitively, in intellectual ecstasy without accompaniment of ideation, at the highest level of conscious being; born of one mother with the vision of God, its life is as it were a flash of blinding light of transmundane origin, impossible to analyze, and yet in the image of our very being."

Neither of the foregoing renderings embodies any foreign matter. On the other hand, only an extended series of alternative renderings would suffice to develop the full reference of the original terms. *Pramātṛ* (from the same root as *pramāṇa*, present also in English "metre") is *quis rationem artis intelligit*; here not as one instructed, but by nature. The notion of innate genius may be compared with Blake's "Man is born like a garden ready planted and sown," and "The knowledge of Ideal Beauty cannot be acquired, it is born with us." But it must be understood that from the Indian point of view, genius is not a fortuitous manifestation, but the necessary consequence of a rectification of the whole personality, accomplished in a previous condition of being; cf. the notion of an absolute *pramāṇa* natural to the Comprehensor, to the Buddha, see note 74, *infra*. The "exaltation of *sattva*" implies, of course, abstraction from extension, operation, local motion (*rajas*), and from indetermination or inertia (*tamas*). Aesthetic experience is a transformation not merely of feeling (as suggested by the word *aesthesis*, *per se*), but equally of understanding; cf. the state of "Deep Sleep," characterized by the expression *prajñāna-ghana-ānanda-mayi*, "a condensed understanding in the mode of ecstasy," discussed below, p. 133 and note 89. The level of pure aesthetic experience is indeed that of the pure angelic understanding, proper to the Motionless Heaven, Brahmaloka. With "like a flash of lightning," cf. *Bṛhadāraṇyaka Upaniṣad*, II, 3, 6 and *Kena Upaniṣad*, 29, where the vision of Brahman is compared to a "sudden flash of lightning," or "What flashes in the lightning." The vision is our very Being, *Ding an Sich*, *svâkāra*, and like our Being, beyond our individually limited grasp (*grahaṇa*) or conception (*saṁkalpa*); "you cannot see the seer of seeing," *Bṛhadāraṇyaka Upaniṣad*, III, 4, 2.[42]

In any case, "It is the spectator's own energy (*utsāha*) that is the cause of tasting, just as when children play with clay elephants"; the permanent mood (*sthāyi-bhāva*) is brought to life as *rasa* because of the spectator's own capacity for tasting, "not by the character or actions of the hero to be imitated (*anukārya*), nor by the deliberate ordering of the work to that end (*tatparatvataḥ*)."[43] Those devoid of the required capacity or energy are no better than the wood or masonry of the gallery.[44] Aesthetic experience is thus only accessible to those competent (*pramātṛ*, *rasika*, *sahṛdaya*). Competence depends "on purity or singleness (*sattva*) of heart and on an inner character (*antara-dharma*) or habit of obedience (*anuśīla*) tending to aversion of attention from external phenomena; this character and habit, not to be acquired by mere learning, but either innate or cultivated, depends on an ideal sensibility (*vāsanā*) and the faculty of self-identification (*yogyatā*) with the forms (*bhavana*) depicted (*varṇanīya*)." [45] Just as the original intuition arose from a self-identification of the artist with the appointed theme, so aesthetic experience, reproduction, arises from a self-identification of the spectator with the presented matter; criticism repeats the process of creation. An interesting case is that of the actor, or any artist, who must not be naturally moved by the passions he depicts, though he may obtain aesthetic experience from the spectacle of his own performance.[46]

Notwithstanding that aesthetic experience is thus declared to be an inscrutable and uncaused spiritual activity, that is virtually ever-present and potentially realizable, but not possible to be realized unless and until all affective and mental barriers have been resolved, all knots of the heart undone, it is necessarily admitted that the experience arises in relation to some specific representation. The elements of this representation, the work of art itself, can be and are discussed by the Hindu rhetoricians at great length, and provide the material and much of the terminology of analysis and criticism. For present purposes it will suffice to present these constituents of the work of art in a brief form; but it must not be forgotten that here only is to be found the tangible (*grāhya*) matter of the work of art, all that can be explained and accounted for in it, and that this all includes precisely that *a priori* knowledge which the spectator must possess or come to possess before he can pretend to competence in the sense above defined. The elements of the work of art are, then:

(1) Determinants (*vibhāva*), viz. the physical stimulants to aesthetic reproduction, particularly the theme and its parts, the indications of time and place, and other apparatus of representation — the whole *factibile*. The operation of the Determinants takes place by the operation of an ideal-sympathy (*sādhāraṇya*), a self-identification with the imagined situation.[47]

(2) Consequents (*anubhāva*), the specific and conventional means of "registering" (*sūcanā*) emotional states, in particular gestures (*abhinaya*).

(3) Moods (*bhāva*), the conscious emotional states as represented in art. These include thirty-three Fugitive or Transient (*vyabhicāri*) Moods such as joy, agitation, impatience, etc., and eight or nine Permanent (*sthāyi*) Moods, the Erotic, Heroic, etc., which in turn are the vehicles of the specific *rasas* or emotional colorings. In any work, one of the Permanent Moods must constitute a master motif to which all the others are subordinate; for "the extended development of a transient emotion becomes an inhibition of *rasa*," [48] or, as we should now express it, the work becomes sentimental, embarrassing rather than moving.

(4) The representation of involuntary physical reactions (*sattva-bhāva*), for example fainting.

All of these determinants and symbols are recognized collectively and indivisibly in aesthetic experience, the work of art being as such a unity; but they are recognized separately in subsequent analysis.

According to the related School of Manifestation (*Vyakti-vāda*) the essential or soul of poetry is called *dhvani*, "the reverberation of meaning arising by suggestion (*vyañjanā*)."[49] In grammar and logic, a word or other symbol is held to have two powers only, those of denotation (*abhidhā*) and connotation (*lakṣaṇā*); for example *gopāla* is literally "cowherd," but constantly signifies Kṛṣṇa. The rhetoricians assume for a word or symbol a third power, that of suggestion (*vyañjanā*), the matter suggested, which we should call the real content of the work, being *dhvani*, with respect to either the theme (*vastu*), any metaphor or other ornament (*alaṁkāra*), or, what is more essential, one of the specific *rasas*. In other words, *abhidhā*, *lakṣaṇā*, and *vyañjanā* correspond to literal, allegorical, and anagogic significance. *Dhvani*, as overtone of meaning, is thus the immediate vehicle of single *rasa* and means to aesthetic experience.[50] Included in *dhvani* is *tātparyārtha*, the meaning conveyed by the whole sentence or formula, as distinct from the mere sum of meanings of its separate parts. The School of Manifestation is so called because the perception (*pratīti*) of *rasa* is thought of simply as the manifestation of an inherent and already existing intuitive condition of the spirit, in the same sense that Enlightenment is virtually ever-present though not always realized. The *pratīti* of *rasa*, as it were, breaks through the enclosing walls (*varaṇa*, *āvaraṇa*) by which the soul, though predisposed by ideal sympathy (*sādhāraṇya*) and sensibility (*vāsanā*), is still immured [51] and restricted from shining forth in its true character as the taster of *rasa* in an aesthetic experience which is as aforesaid the very twin brother of the experience of the unity of Brahman.

In the later and otherwise more synthetic scheme of the *Sāhitya Darpaṇa*, the *rasa* and *dhvani* theories are not quite so closely linked, *dhvani* being now not so much the soul of all poetry as characteristic of the superior sort of poetry in which what is suggested outweighs what is literally expressed.

For the sake of completeness there need only be mentioned two earlier theories in which Ornament or Figures (*alaṁkāra*) and Style or Composition (*rīti*) are regarded respectively as the essential elements in art. These theories, which have not held their own in India, may be compared to the minor European conceptions of art as dexterity, or as consisting merely of aesthetic surfaces which are significant only as sources of sensation. This last point of view can be maintained consistently in India only from the standpoint of the naïve realism which underlies a strictly monastic prejudice against the world.

It remains to be pointed out that the *rasa* and *dhvani* theories are essentially metaphysical and Vedântic in method and conclusion, though they are expressed not so much in terms of the pure Vedânta of the Upaniṣads as in those of a later Vedânta combined with other systems, particularly the Yoga. The fully evolved Indian theory of beauty is in fact hardly to be dated before the tenth or eleventh century, though the doctrine of *rasa* is already clearly enunciated in Bharata's *Nāṭya Śāstra*, which may be anterior to the fifth century and itself derives from still older sources.

In any case, the conception of the work of art as determined outwardly to use and inwardly to a delight of the reason; the view of its operation as not intelligibly causal, but by way of a destruction of the mental and affective barriers behind which the natural manifestation of the spirit is concealed; the necessity that the soul should be already prepared for this emancipation by an inborn or acquired sensibility; the requirement of self-identification with the ultimate theme, on the part of both artist and spectator, as prerequisite to visualization in the first instance and reproduction in the second; finally, the conception of ideal beauty as unconditioned by natural affections, indivisible, supersensual, and indistinguishable from the gnosis of God—all these characteristics of the theory demonstrate its logical connection with the predominant trends of Indian thought, and its natural place in the whole body of Indian philosophy.

Consequently, though it could not be argued that any aesthetic theory is explicitly set forth in the Upaniṣads, it will not surprise us to find that the ideas and terminology of the later aesthetic are there already recognizable. For example, in the *Bṛhadāraṇyaka Upaniṣad*, I, 4, 7, the world is said to be differentiated or known in plurality by, and only by, means of name and aspect, *nāmarūpa*, idea and image; *ibid.*, III, 2, 3 and 5, "Voice (*vāc*) is an apprehender (*graha*); it is seized by the idea (*nāma*) as an over-apprehender, then indeed by voice (*vāc*) one utters thoughts (*nāmāni*)," and similarly "Sight (*cakṣu*) is an apprehender; it is seized by aspect (*rūpa*) as an over-apprehender, then indeed by the eye (*cakṣu*) one sees things (*rūpāṇi*)."[52] Further, *ibid.*, III, 9, 20, "on the heart (*hṛdaya*) are aspects (*rūpāṇi*) based," and similarly in the case of speech. As to the heart, "it is the same as Prajāpati, it is Brahman," *ibid.*, V, 3, and "other than that Imperishable, there is none that (really) sees," *ibid.*, III, 8, 11.[53] Actual objects (*rūpāṇi*) seen in space are really seen not as such, but only as colored areas, the concept of space being altogether mental and conventional.[54]

The Indian theory, in origins and formulation, seems at first sight to be *sui generis*. But merely because of the specific idiomatic and mythical form in which it finds expression, it need not be thought of as otherwise than universal. It does not in fact differ from what is implicit in the Far Eastern view of art, or on the other hand in any essentials from the Scholastic Christian point of view, or what is asserted in the aphorisms of Blake; it does differ essentially from the modern non-intellectual interpretations of art as sensation. What are probably the most significant elements in the Asiatic theory are the views (1) that aesthetic experience is an ecstasy in itself inscrutable, but in so far as it can be defined, a delight of the reason, and (2) that the work of art itself, which serves as the stimulus to the release of the spirit from all inhibitions of vision, can only come into being and have being as a thing ordered to specific ends. Heaven and Earth are united in the analogy (*sādṛśya*, etc.) of art, which is an ordering of sensation to intelligibility and tends toward an ultimate perfection in which the seer perceives all things imaged in himself.

Chapter II

MEISTER ECKHART'S VIEW OF ART

Chapter II

MEISTER ECKHART'S VIEW OF ART

Docti rationem artis intelligunt, indocti voluptatem.
Quintilian, IX, 4.

THE Schoolmen composed no special treatise with the title 'Philosophy of Art.' . . . There is nevertheless a far-reaching theory of art to be found in their writings."[55] Amongst such there are none more universal, more profound, or more distinguished by vigor of statement and clarity of thought than those of Meister Eckhart,[56] whose *Sermons* might well be termed an Upaniṣad of Europe. Eckhart's preëminence is not of the order of genius; what is remarkable in him is nothing in kind, nothing individual or curious, but only a great energy or will that allows him to resume and concentrate in one consistent demonstration the spiritual being of Europe at its highest tension. Toward his theme he is utterly devout, and his trained mental powers are the author of his style, but otherwise, in his own words spoken with reference to the painter of portraits, "it is not himself that it reveals to us" (37); "What I give out is in me . . . as the gift of God" (143).

The real analogy between Eckhart's modes of thought and those which have long been current in India should make it easy for the Vedântist or Mahāyāna Buddhist to understand him, which would require a much greater effort on the part of a Protestant Christian or modern philosopher. In European readers, some knowledge of Scholastic thought and Christian theology must be taken for granted. Partly for the sake of Indian readers, and partly because the use of Oriental side by side with European technical terms cannot much longer be avoided by students of aesthetics or metaphysics, I have bracketed Sanskrit equivalents wherever they serve to explain or better define the meaning. For the rest, every word or passage enclosed by quotation marks is Eckhart's. I have not thought it necessary to distinguish his own words from those of the various doctors, masters, and heathen philosophers whom he sometimes quotes and endorses, this not being a study of Eckhart's sources. I have tried to arrange the available material logically, and where it has been necessary to develop the idea, to do so strictly in harmony with Scholastic ideas in general and Eckhart's phrases in particular, often using his own words even when this is not specifically indicated by the page references.

Eckhart's whole conception of human life in operation and attainment is aesthetic: it runs through all his thought that man is an artist in the analogy of the "exalted workman," and his idea of "sovran good" and "immutable delight" is that of a perfected art.[57] Art is religion, religion art, not related, but the same. No one can study theology without perceiving this; for example, the Trinity is an "arrangement" of God,[58] "articulate speech" (369), "determined by formal notions" (268), "symmetry with supreme lucidity" (366). Eckhart is writing, not a treatise on the arts as such, though he is evidently quite familiar with them, but sermons on the art of knowing God. Ignorance is "lack of knowledge . . . brutish" (13).

What is knowledge? Threefold: (1) of particulars and generals, sensible, empirical, literal, indicative, *saṁvyavahārika-pratyakṣa*, (2) of universals, rational or intelligible, allegorical, conventional, *parokṣa*, (3) of sameness, without image or likeness, transcendental, anagogic, *aparokṣa* = *paramârthika-pratyakṣa* (13, 32, 87–88, 166, 228, II, 183, etc.; cf. Chapter V). Of these the first two (*avidyā*) are relative, the last (*vidyā*) immediate and absolute, only to be expressed in terms of negation.

To clarify his meaning, Eckhart makes constant allusion to the practice of specific arts, to the art in the artist, and to the perfecting of art and artist. Understanding may be audibly or visibly perceived, in either case as an aesthetic process. For example, "I see the lilies in the field, their gaiety, their color, all their leaves" (143), just as any brute perceives them; this is simply the recognition and relishing of "creatures as creatures," "as they are in themselves," to be recognized and valued as to their uses. But "my inner man relishes things not as creatures but as the gift of God" (143), that is, as intelligible images, here with a specifically edifying connotation. "And again, to my innermost man they savor not of God's gift but of ever and aye. Even so do all creatures speak God" (143), "I am come like the fragrance of a flower" (284); that is the overtone of meaning, suggestion, *dhvani*, unalloyed savoring, *rasa*. In all, these are the three aesthetic functions of denotation, connotation, and implication, corresponding to recognition, interpretation, and immediate understanding.

The soul has two powerful faculties, intellect and will, expressed in vision and love, which can be exercised in fruitful operation, outwardly or inwardly (166). Where things exist as intelligible images, as means of understanding and communication, intellectually, in the imagination, there lies man's way. It is here that things are known in unintelligible multiplicity and must be realized in intelligible unity, here that the use of things is understood, and that renunciation of all uses must be made: "to find nature herself all her likenesses have to be shattered and the further in the nearer the actual thing" (259), such renunciation and such shattering being of the essence of art, in which all things are seen alike without any sense of possession, not in their nature but in their being, quite disinterestedly.[59]

In outward operation, these powers of the soul, intellect and will, correspond to vocation, as with the artist (artifex), professor (doctor), or celebrant (priest), and to conduct as distinguished from specific skill. The artist is not a special kind of man, but every man is a special kind of artist. The vocations ("arranging this or that," 16) are so many different disciplines; conduct ("comforting another," 16) another discipline proper to all men alike. Every activity involves what we should now call an aesthetic process, a succession of problem, solution, and execution. Materials apart, whoever acts, acts in the same way, will following the intellect, whether he makes a house, or studies mathematics, or performs an office, or does good works.

Our modern system of thought has substituted for this division of labor a spiritual caste system which divides men into species. Those who have lost most by this are the artists, professionally speaking, on the one hand, and laymen generally on the other. The artist (meaning such as would still be so called) loses by his isolation and corresponding pride, and by the emasculation of his art, no longer conceived as intellectual, but only as emotional in motivation and significance; the workman (to whom the name of artist is now denied) loses in that he is not called, but forced to labor unintelligently, goods being valued above men. All alike have lost, in that art being now a luxury, no longer the normal type of all activity, all men are compelled to live in squalor and disorder and have become so inured to this that they are unaware of it. The only surviving artists in the Scholastic, Gothic sense, are scientists, surgeons, and engineers, the only ateliers, laboratories.

Just because Eckhart's treatment of aesthetics is not *ad hoc*, but takes for granted the point of view of a school, not in any private sense his own, it has a special value; we can have no doubt that it was actually in this fashion that cultured men in Paris and Cologne, in the twelfth and thirteenth centuries, when Christian art was at its zenith, thought of art and the specific arts. These same men in their collective capacity as the Church prescribed the themes of art and the more essential details of its iconography; the workman, sometimes a trained monk, more often a trained gildsman, added from the storehouse of tradition another element to form besides the skill of craft which he was expected to practice in his vocation. Thus intellect and will worked in unanimity. Is not the determination of this art — that in it which alone is common to the mind and to the product, that is, its imagery, not its style, still less any individual mannerism — a thing that must be understood if we would understand Christian art at all? I sometimes wonder if we really want to understand it. For on the one hand, from the histories of art one would suppose that the very form by which the art is moved from within can be neglected, and that nothing matters in it but the facts of history, accidents of provenance and influence, and problems of attribution — all those things with which the mediaeval workman was least of all concerned; and on the other hand, we have those who insist that the enjoyment of the work of art, admittedly its ultimate value (if we understand "enjoyment" rightly, which is the very problem of aesthetics, and cannot be assumed) demands no other preparatory discipline, being an unintelligible ecstasy (as may be granted), and can be taught (which is inadmissible) to those who aspire to the transcendent vision, but are only too ready to be persuaded that the mirror of the universe is the eye's intrinsic faculty (such readiness is "a trick the soul has, when indulging in comfortable intuitions of divinity," 447). The study of art, from a historical point of view, may be harmless in itself, yet no better than the satisfaction of a curiosity; the enjoyment of works of art merely as a pleasure of the eye or ear may be harmless in itself ("that a disagreeable noise should be as grateful to the ear as the sweet tones of a lyre is a thing I never shall attain to," II, 97), yet no more than an enhanced sensation. If this were all, aesthetic would be nothing more than a discussion of taste, and so indeed the experimental psychologists believe.

To speak of art exclusively in terms of sensation is doing violence to the inner man, the knowing subject; to extract from Eckhart's thought a theory of taste (*ruci*) would be doing violence to its unity. If I venture at all to extract from it a theory of art, this is not as an exercise in dialectics, but because it is required for the specific interpretation of Christian art, and because the Scholastic view is more than a great provincial school of thought; it represents a universal mode of thought, and this mode throws a light on the analogous theories that have prevailed in Asia, and should serve Western students as a means of approach to, and understanding of, Asiatic art.

The doctrine of types, ideas, forms, or images is of fundamental importance for the understanding of Eckhart's references to art. More rarely, the words semblance, likeness, symbol, effigy, pattern, and prototype are employed. Amongst all these, type and prototype, pattern, idea, and ideal are used only with reference to things known and seen intellectually (*parokṣa*), the others in the same sense or with reference to the image materially embodied (*pratyakṣa*). To begin with, what is an image in these two senses? An image "is anything known or born" (258), or anything both known and born or made. The Son, for example, is the Father's "own image abiding in himself . . . his immanent form," and at the same time "the exact likeness, the perfect image of his Father" (258) in a distinct Person. In the same way all creatures "in their preëxisting forms in God have been divine life for ever," only their material embodiment "when Nature is working in time and space" (71) being by birth and as it were God's handiwork: "these preëxisting forms are the origin or principle of the creation of all creatures, and in this sense they are types and pertain to practical knowledge" (253). They live in the "divine mind," the "hoard" which "is God's art" (461): "Intellect is the temple of God wherein he is shining in all his glory. Nowhere does God dwell more really than in this temple of his intellect's nature" (212) (*ālaya-vijñāna*), "quiddity or mode is the way into this temple" (*ibid.*). And like God's hoard "There is a power in the soul called mind (*vijñāna, saṁkalpa*); it is her storehouse of incorporeal forms and intellectual notions" (402); the ideas in this storehouse of the soul may seem either to be new or to be remembered (105), but in either case are as it were recollected (226, 295), for "all the words of his divine essence flow into the word in our mind in distinction of Person just as memory pours out treasure of images into the powers of the soul" (402). Another superficial distinction of ideas in kind can be made as between the ideas of natural species, as when one works with the "rose-form" (251) or the image of Conrad (128), and artificial ideas, arising "theoretically, as the house of wood and stone is designed in the architect's practical mind, who makes the house as much like his ideal as he can" (252), either kind being "in the practical power" as the "idea of the work" (252) to be done, if work is to be done, as well as abiding in the mind as objects of understanding and *a priori* means of rational communication. Either of these kinds of ideas is equally invention (*anuvitta*), a discovery amongst "the sum of all the forms conceived by man and which subsist in God himself, I having no property in them and no idea of ownership" (35, cf. 17); which point of view we all naturally endorse when we say that an idea has come to us, or that we have hit upon it, *eureka*, never that we have made it. At the best, we have prepared ourselves for it by emptying our conscience of all other creature images and fugitive emotions, accepting for the time being only the seal or imprint of this one thing. So the image is in the artist, not he in it; it is his whose image it is, not his who harbors it (52). When we find "just as the artist, inspired by his art, will carve in wood or paint on canvas or the wall" (II, 211), "art" means the idea of the theme, as it presents itself to him. The image in the object, in the artist's mind, and in the graven image are the same, though in the artist and in his work only according to his powers, not in its full perfection. In the graven image of anything it may be thought of not as introduced by the artist but as latent in the medium because of the appetite for form that matter has; for example, "when the artist makes a statue out of wood or stone he does not put the image in the wood, he chips away the wood which hides the form. He gives the wood nothing, he takes it away: carves it out where it is too thick, pares off overlay, and then there appears what was hidden" (II, 82) — an analogy of how God's image is ever present in the ground of the soul, but concealed by veils and hindrances (II, 81).

God's and man's ideas or types are thus not Platonic ideas external to intellect (in Essence there is no likeness or image, but only Sameness, *samatā*), nor immutable or general, but types of activity, forces, principles of work or becoming, living and particular — "to call a tree a tree is not to name it, for all the species are confused" (117), no two creatures being alike in their nature, for "every creature makes innate denial; the one denies it is the other" (249). Ideas are as many in number as there have been or ever can be things in time, "there are as many types as there are grades of nature to be typified" (252, 253); they cannot be more in number than this, because God's work is not by choice, there is nothing that he leaves undone, what he thinks is, what is is what he thinks, his creation is without means or succession. "Every nature emanates from its appropriate form" (477), but our conception of process and succession is merely "due to our gross senses" (365);

from God's point of view ideas are all known at once in perfection and in one form; from our temporal point of view ideas are free and variably becoming, or as we now say evolving. From any point of view, ideas or forms (*nāma*) are "living," not merely existing like standards fixed and deposited for safe-keeping — ideas not merely of static shapes, but ideas of acts (16).

"An icon in stone or on the wall, with no foundation to it (that is, materials apart, and) taken simply as form, is the same form as his whose form it is" (64). So then normally there will be nothing of the artist in the work except his skill: "the painter who has painted a good portrait therein shows his art; it is not himself that it reveals to us" (37). But if the painter paints his own portrait, as God does, then both his skill and his image will be in it, himself as he knows himself, but not his very self: "this reflects credit on the painter who embodies in it his dearest conception of his art and makes it the image of himself. The likeness of the portrait praises the author without words" (97). "If I paint my likeness on the wall, he who sees the likeness is not seeing me; but anyone who sees me sees my likeness and not my likeness merely but my child. If I really knew my soul, anyone who saw my conception of it would say it was my son, for I share therewith my energy and nature, and as here so it is in the Godhead. The Father understands himself perfectly clearly, so there appears to him his image, that is to say, his Son" (408) (the portrait and the corporeal man are both the man's conception of himself, they are "alike" in form, however different in aspect flesh and paint must be).

In this connection may be considered a difficult passage occurring in the exegesis of Genesis I, 26, "Let us make man in our image and likeness." Eckhart says, "Work comes from the outward and from the inner man, but the innermost man takes no part in it. In making a thing the very innermost self of a man comes into outwardness" (195), in which there seems to be some contradiction. The first is clear: the work as a substance in a given shape comes from the man's hands molding matter, and as form from the specific idea in him, as it is in his intellect, which does no work in molding matter, but only singles out the best it can according to its idiosyncrasy. Because the actual handiwork is done by the man's very body, it is only natural that there should be a trace of his physiognomy left in it, just as the axe which "brings about the workman's desired end" (II, 178) leaves its mark in the wood and could be identified thereby.[59] So then in touch and style the work somewhat reveals the man, that is as to the accidents of his being. That the very innermost self of a man also "comes into outwardness," according to Eckhart's own analogy, as "When God made man the very innermost heart of the Godhead was concerned in his making" (195, 436), and yet "God's works enclose a mere nothing of God, wherefore they cannot disclose him" (87, cf. *Bhagavad Gītā*, IX, 4 and 5). Or again, "Form is a revelation of essence" (38), in which there is neither image nor likeness; essence is in all things, and though it "gets not," yet "it moves movable things like creatures" (284). As Godhead to God, so is innermost man to workman, Godhead and innermost man being present in the work, one in being with it, but not operatively or intelligibly. In Eckhart's own work we see the man possessed of his ideas, and wrestling with his means, the "intractable" (119) and untaught German speech of his day; but in the ideas at last so vigorously expressed there is a "mere nothing of the man" as he is in God. For man to be in his handiwork as God is in his creation it would have to be as immanent life, the thing made would have to be alive and possessed of free will. If we do sometimes say that a work lives, this is only metaphorical, a sort of animism which projects our own living reactions into the thing as it is in itself.

That there is no life in man's handiwork underlies the Muḥammadan doctors' interdiction of representative art, the imitation of living forms being regarded as a blasphemy, inasmuch as the artist brings into being a pseudo-creation, as it were in mockery of God, who alone gives life. Nevertheless, as we have seen and shall further demonstrate, Christian art is not a mimicry of natural species, nor merely a source of pleasurable sensations, but is a manner of speaking about God and Nature: it no more trespasses upon God's dignity than when we speak of him or see of him or taste of him, using names or other images,[60] being only too well aware the while that "nothing true can be spoken of God" (8), "God is nameless" (246), "there is no knowing him by likeness" (55), (who is *nirābhāsa*, *amūrta*), "a portrait of the highest seraph limned in black would be a better likeness far than God portrayed as highest seraph; that were a preëminent unlikeness" (46), and yet believing that there is nothing "more useful and salutary to the soul than excursions in the science of the holy Trinity and unity" (392) in which excursions we are naturally compelled to make use of name and form, being "permitted to use the names his saints have called him by" (70, cf. St Thomas, *Sum. Theol.*, I, Q. 51, A. 3, "it is in no wise contrary to truth for intelligible things to be set forth in Scripture under sensible figures, since it is not said for the purpose of maintaining that intelligible things are sensible, but in order that properties of intelligible things may be understood according to similitude through sensible figures"). The demonstration of iconoclasm is as follows: "they held their peace for fear of lying" (237); "Anyone content with what can be expressed in words — God is a word, Heaven is a word — is aptly styled an unbeliever" (339). But this is a sort of asceticism or renunciation proper only to those who have a vision of God without means and have earned the right to say that all scripture is vain; otherwise, a denial of the soul's powers, expressed in outward works, as a means to edification and enlightenment, is by no means excusable.

Notwithstanding that man's handiwork is without life, still the human maker is an analogy of the "exalted workman" (376), the divine architect, all-maker (Viśvakarma). "Suppose some master of the arts. If he produces a work of art he none the less preserves his arts within himself: the arts are the artist in the artist" (that is, in the man so called), just as "Things flowed forth finite into time while abiding in eternity" where they are "God in God" (285). "The idea of the work exists in the worker's practical mind as an object of his understanding, which regards it as expressing his idea to which he forms the material work" (252), that is, not in his mind as a *mode* of understanding, but as a thing already and directly understood, for "I make a letter of the alphabet like the image of that letter in my mind, not like my mind itself" (235). Every least detail of the work will correspond to details of form in the artist's mind: "no architect can carry in his head the plan of a whole house without the plans of all its details" (252).

Again, "the form, idea, or semblance of a thing, a rose, for instance, is present in my soul, and must be for two reasons. One is because from the appearance of its mental form (*jñāna-sattva-rūpa*) I can paint the rose in corporal matter, so there must be an image of the rose-form in my soul. The second reason is because from the subjective rose-idea I recognize the objective rose although I do not copy it (that is, do not copy the rose in painting). Just as I can carry in my mind the notion of a house I never mean to build" (252). "For the purpose of making a crock a man takes a handful of clay; that is the medium he works in. He gives it a form he has in him, nobler than his material" (68). And as to this form as it exists in the artist's mind, "Another power in the soul is that wherewith she thinks (*dhī, dhyai*). This power is able to picture in itself things which are not there, so that I can see things as well as with my eyes, or even better. I can see a rose in winter when there are no roses (cf. 116), therefore with this power the soul produces (*ākarṣati*) things from the non-existent (*hṛdaya-ākāśa*) like God who creates things out of nothing (*kha* = χάος)" (212, cf. 445). In any case "to be properly expressed a thing must proceed from within, moved by its form; it must come, not in from without, but out from within" (108).

In other words, just as "the soul is the form of the body," so the art in the artist is the form of the work: "the cutting of the wood is from the saw; but that it assumes at length the form of a bed is from the design of the art" (in the artist), "the form of the bed is not in the saw or the axe, but a certain movement toward that form," St Thomas, *Sum. Theol.*, I, Q. 110. A. 2 and Q. 118, A. 1, quoting also Avicenna, "all forms which are in matter proceed from the concept of the intellect."

The arising of the image is not by an act of will whether human or divine, but of attention (*dhāraṇā*) when the will is at rest; there can be nothing meritorious (17) in the possession of images, since an image "receives its being from the thing whose image it is, for it is a natural product . . . prior to the will, will following the image" (51, cf. 17). The aesthetic process is as follows: what I say "springs up in me, then I pause in the idea, and thirdly I speak it out" (222), or again, "First when a word is conceived in my mind it is a subtle, intangible thing; it is a true word when it takes shape in my thought. Later, as spoken aloud by my mouth, it is but an outward expression of the interior word" (80), "the mind sees and formulates and the will wills and memory holds it fast" (16). As to this abiding intention, or pause in the idea, "my wish of today is my purpose of tomorrow, the idea of which is kept alive (*sthita*) by my actual thinking (*vibhāvayati*) of it, just as, they said, God's works are done" (238). As to the work, "Working and becoming are the same. When the carpenter stops working, the house will stop becoming. Still the axe and stop the growth" (163); "Man requires many instruments for his external works; much preparation is needed ere he can bring them forth as he has imagined them" (5); the seeking intellect "spends perhaps a year or more in research on some natural fact, finding out what it is, only to work as long again stripping off what it is not" (17), but "angels . . . need less means for their works and have fewer images" (5).

As we have seen, the aesthetic process is threefold, the arising of the idea in germ, its taking shape before the mind's eye, and outward expression in work (80, 228). The first act is necessarily the effect of attention directed to a given object: the artist is commissioned, not to paint, but to paint something in particular, let us say a flower or an angel (*deva*) or other object. Eckhart takes the case of the host of angels, and though he does not refer to the third stage of actual execution, this would be an easy step. "A master was once questioned by his pupil about the angelic order. He answered him and said, Go hence and withdraw into thyself until thou understandest: give thy whole self up to it, then look, refusing to see anything but what thou findest there. It will seem to thee at first as though thou art the angels with them and as thou dost surrender to their collective being thou shalt think thyself [61] the angels as a whole with the whole company of angels" (216). So far, the process is identical with the Indian imager's *dhyāna-yoga*: and had an actual picture of the angels been required, it might have been added *dhyātvā kuryāt*, that is, "Having thus seen and surrendered to the presented form, begin the work." Had the painting been required to fill a given space, or had it been intended that the angels should stand in some particular relation to other figures in the picture, all this, being a part of the prescribed object, would have had its prototype in the perfected mental image. As to the picture itself, if one had been made, it is merely an arrangement of pigments, nor can my eye learn anything about the angels from its sensations of reflected light: only *I* can have some idea of them, and that not in or by sensation, but by their image, the same that was in the artist's mind, and now taken back from the picture into my mind, for "bodily hearing and sight are engineered in the mind" (93) and "If my soul knows an angel she knows him by some means and in an image, an image imageless, not in an image such as they are here" (112). "Before my eye can see the painting on the wall it must be filtered through the air and in a still more tenuous form borne into my phantasy to be assimilated by my understanding" (111).

Thus the artist's model is always a mental image. The eye (*māṁsa-cakṣu*) is nothing but a mirror: *it* may be said to see an object, such as a rose or stone or work of art, by virtue of some substantial kinship between them (104, 105, 116, 152, 212, 240); "it is a case of like to like" (258). But if I say *I* see, it is only as it were, for "If it were intellect, I should see nothing" (105). "I see" only indirectly and by means of the eye as instrument, which instrument serves me because of a corresponding soul power linked to it, but far removed from matter (104); "subtract the mind, and the eye is open to no purpose" (288). My eye sees flat, but I see in relief; this relief is not necessarily a fact, but an idea of relation, which would have validity for me even supposing a total unreality of the external world. The inwardly known aspect (*antarjñeya-rūpa*), relatively immaterial, is the means by which I recognize what the eye sees, the only means by which I can pretend to understand what the eye reports, or with which I can speak of it to others. "I do not see the hand, the stone, itself; I see the image of the stone, but I do not see this image in a second image or by any other means; I see it without means and without image. This image is itself the means: image without image like motion without motion although causing motion and size which has no size though the principle of size" (114). "The soul knows only in effigy" (243), not anything in itself, but more nearly as things are in God, ideally. I can never see what my eye sees (sensibly) nor hear what my ear hears as vibration, I can only know rationally, by means of an image. "We can see the sunlight where it falls upon a tree or any other object, but we fail to apprehend the sun itself" (72) except as an idea. There is nothing exotic in this point of view; it is an axiom of modern science, which knows matter only in mathematical formulae, not in sensation.

From all this it will be understood how from the Scholastic point of view a naturalistic or visual art, made only according to the eyes (this means, made to yield sensations as nearly as possible identical with those evoked by the model itself), and only for the eyes, must be regarded not merely as irreligious or idolatrous (idolatry is the love of creatures as they are in themselves), but also irrational and indeterminate. For the only thing which can be truly likened to the natural species is its reflection in the mirror of the eye, which is a sensation, not an understanding (the eye, having no understanding of its own, remains incomprehensible to intellect, a case of unlike to unlike). Again, the material image, the work of art, is commensurable with natural species only as to substance (both are essence, but essence cannot be measured): fundamentally incommensurable, in difference of material and life. Nature and art are alike (*sādṛśya*) only in idea, otherwise irreconcilable.

Recognizability, whether of natural species or material image, has nothing to do with any fancied likeness between these two, but is by means of the incorporeal form or image (*nāma*) which is in the object, in the artist, in the work of art, and finally in the spectator, having been brought into visibility as far as possible in the material image (*rūpa*) in another nature, but still not made of that nature. Just in so far as anything could be made like natural species, that is self-moving which is inconceivable, or as Muḥammadans would say forbidden, it would not be art but Nature, or necromancy at the best; or could the artist, which is conceivable potentially, though it may be temporally impossible, attain perfection, becoming one with God, he would share in God's creation from time everlasting, natural species would be his image in time as they are God's, nothing would remain but the ever-present world-picture as God sees it. There would be no occasion for works of art, the end of art having been accomplished. In the meantime, where we find ourselves, an art made as far as possible according to the eye's intrinsic faculty (253) and merely for the eye can be thought of only as a superposition of illusion upon illusion, a willing substitution of the snake for the rope, Eckhart's own metaphor of double illusion being that of a straight shaft seen in the water as if bent (II, 77).

In what sense art is necessarily conventional or rational he expresses thus: "What the eye sees has to be conveyed to it (the soul) by means, in images" (111, cf. 82). The skilful painter can "do Conrad to the life" (128), but what is doing Conrad to the life? Not making something that could be mistaken for the man himself, but making "the very image of him" (*ibid.*), that is, as far as lies in the painter's power, his "express image" (253) as it exists reflected in the mirror of God's essence, "the exemplary element in him (Conrad) which is on a par with God," "a matter of likeness of form" (157). "Will enjoys things as they are in themselves, whereas intellect enjoys them as they are in it. . . . The eye in itself is a better thing than the eye as painted on the wall. Nevertheless, I still maintain that intellect is higher than the will" (213). He means in that it sees things somewhat as God sees them, *sub specie aeternitatis* (47), at their source, impartially; for "Creatures all come into my mind and are rational in me. I alone prepare all creatures to return to God"; "I alone take all creatures out of their sense into my mind and make them one in me" (143); "Intellect (*manas, prajñā*) raises all things up into God" (86). "Creatures never rest till they have gotten into human nature; therein do they attain to their original form, God namely" (380), human nature having "nothing to do with time" (206). "The most trivial thing perceived in God, a flower for example as espied in God (that is, in its and His true and single aspect, *svarūpa*), would be a thing more perfect than the universe" (206) as it is in itself. It is as artist, seeing rationally or formally, that man sees things in their perfection and eternal youth, as far as his idiosyncrasy permits, "as far as the recipient will allow" (212).

Naturalism in art has nothing to do with subject-matter in itself. An image of God may be made repulsive in its suggestion of actuality; a painting of a flower may be like nothing on earth. Eckhart holds no brief for any one formula, as for hieratic art or art profane with respect to theme. "He who seeks God under settled forms lays hold of the form while missing the God concealed in it" (49), is really an idolater. Sacred subjects are no more valid images of God than are the forms of natural species: "Eight heavens are spoken of and nine choirs of angels . . . you must know that expressions of that sort, which conjure up pictures in the mind, merely serve as allurements to God" (328), and as "Augustine says, 'All scripture is vain'" (69). Again and again Eckhart insists that all content (not all intent) is God, one should learn to see him anywhere and everywhere: "to whom God is dearer in one thing than another, that man is a barbarian, still in the wilds, a child" (419), "finding God in one way rather than another . . . is not the best," "we should be able to enjoy him in any guise and in any thing" (482, 483), "what e'er it be" (419), "I am come like the fragrance of a flower" (284), "any flea as it is in God is nobler than the highest of the angels in himself" (240). This is the perfected impartiality of art; the angelic (*adhidaivata*) point of view, wherein all things are loved alike, "in itself everything is lovable, and nothing hateful," Dante, *Convivio*, IV, 1, 25.

So much for the artist's mode of understanding, intellectual or rational. The work of art, man's "creature," is by the same token, even more than by its substantial distinction from the object, conventional; to be interpreted and understood not as a direct reflection of the world as the world is in itself, but as a symbol or group of symbols having an ascertained rational significance and an even deeper content, not functioning only as means to recognition but as means to communication and to vision. Thus with reference to the interpretation of scripture and myths in general, and the same holds good for any other kind of art, "the material things in them, they say, must be translated to a higher plane. . . . All the stories taken from them have another, esoteric meaning. Our understanding of them is as totally unlike the thing as it is in itself and as it is in God as though it did not exist" (257), but there is more in the work of art than can be understood, "none so wise but when he tries to fathom them will find they are beyond his depth and discover more therein" (*ibid.*). Art is simultaneously denotation, connotation, and suggestion; statement, implication, and content; literal, allegorical, and anagogic.

If art is thus by nature rational, why is not every work of art immediately intelligible? Just because the artist sees only just so much and what of the express image his powers permit; man's images are a specific selection from an inexhaustible sum of possibilities. "Words *derive* their power from the original Word" (99), such selections being differently made in different ages, by different races, and to a less marked degree by different individuals. As constantly asserted by Scholastic philosophy, the thing known is in the knower according to the mode of the knower: therefore "All souls have not the same aptitude . . . vision . . . is not enjoyed the same by all" (301). "Art amounts, in temporal things, to singling out the best" (461),[62] that is, the most essential from any given point of view, which may be yours or mine, or may have been that of the first or thirteenth century, or that of any other given environment and heritage. That is why in art, even when the same subject has been dealt with, or the same natural species "imitated," we find an unending variety of treatment, constituting what we call styles. Differences of spoken language are the most obvious example of this; but he greatly deludes himself who thinks that any of the arts is a universal language, or that the language of any art is by nature onomatopoetic. The variety of styles, and what has often been called progress and decadence in art but is really the historical procession of the styles, have nothing to do with man's varying and always very limited ability to mimic nature. Styles are idioms of knowledge and communication. They suffice for communication in so far and for so long as they are understood by convention (*saṁketa*); elsewhere or at another time, they must be learnt before the art can be deciphered, which requires "industry and patience," "just as one learns to write" (10, 9), or as "calling requires the uses of discrimination" (II, 93).

We have divined that style or idiom represents a particular modality or partiality of vision; the lineaments (*lakṣaṇas*) of which modality are determined by the relation between the artist individually and his theme (cf. *Śukranītisāra*, IV, 4, 159–160); and as this relation is unique and reflects the powers and limitations of the individual, the mode of pattern in his mind may be called his own. The accidents of being by which an individuality is recognized may indeed be called a man's own, man as he is in himself; "my looks are not my nature, they are accidents of nature" (94), "accidents are various" (253). In this sense every artist leaves in all his work something of himself, and "Supposing God had called in any angel to help in the making of the soul he must have put into the soul something of the angel, for never did an artist paint, carve an image or write the letters of the alphabet, but he must have copied the pattern in *his* mind" (II, 203), and not the pattern in the universal mind, individual intellect having "in no wise the perfection nor plenitude for it" (17). Style is not convention as principle, though all styles and all art are conventional, or as Eckhart says "rational": style is a particular body of convention as distinguished from other bodies. If then style is the man, as has been said with some measure of truth, this does not mean that style is in itself a virtue, or an occasion for pride. Touch and style are the accidents of art. As Chuang Tzŭ expresses it, the limits of things are their own limits in so far as they are things. In so far as art transcends style, we call it universal: Bach surpasses Beethoven. God has no style, *his* "idiosyncrasy is being" (206).

In intellect, which, as Eckhart so often insists, is the summit, head, or highest power of the soul, whereby it touches the consciousness of God, man and God are like, but in abiding intention (*kratu*) and in working (*karma*) most unlike, for here enter in the elements of will and time.

Man's ideas live in his mind only for so long, even though it be all his life (238); but creatures have been alive in God for ever, and ever shall be, though in themselves alive only by birth at a given time (352, cf. *Pañcaviṁśa Brāhmaṇa*, VI, 9, 18). And in the case of causes of becoming other than the first cause, such causes "can with safety quit the things they cause when these have gotten being of their own. When the house is in being its builder can depart and for the reason that it is not the builder alone that makes the house: the materials thereof he draws from Nature. But God provides creature with the whole of what it is, so he is bound to stay with it or it will promptly drop out of existence" (427), "as a picture is painted upon canvas, and it fades" (237); similarly "Augustine observes that the architect who builds a house therein displays his art; though it may fall to ruin the art within his soul neither ages nor decays" (129).

With respect to his "staying with creatures to keep them in being" (427, cf. 261) Eckhart thinks of God as a mother (the creations both of God and man are in the nature of children begotten and conceived), and it will not be overlooked that in so far as man takes care of things that have been made and preserves them from decay, he is working temporally in the analogy of God's maternal maintenance. All man's working in creation, preservation, and destruction is a temporal analogy of God's simultaneous expression, maintenance, and resolution, *sṛṣṭi*, *sthiti*, *laya*. But "yonder no work is done at all" (238); "if the carpenter were perfect at his work he would not need materials; he would no sooner think a house than, lo, it would be made," as is the case "with works in God; he thinks them and behold they are" (238); or again, "a carpenter building a house will first erect it in his mind and, were the house enough subject to his will, then, materials apart, the only difference between them would be that of begetter and suddenly begotten . . . (as) it is in God . . . one God, there being no distinction of outpouring (*abhisṛṣṭi*) and outpoured (*abhisarga*)" (72).[63]

Alike in man and God, the "art" (intuition-expression) is and remains wholly in the artist; but "think not it is with God as with a human carpenter, who works or works not as he chooses, who can do or leave undone at his good pleasure. It is not thus with God; but finding thee ready, he is obliged to act, to overflow into thee; just as the sun must needs burst forth when the air is bright, and is unable to contain itself" (23). The "being ready" is otherwise expressed as matter's being "insatiable for form" (18); so God "must do, willy-nilly" (162), according to his nature, without a why. In man this becomes what has been called the gratuitousness of art: "man ought not to work for any why, not for God nor for his glory nor for anything at all that is outside him, but only for that which is his being, his very life within him" (163, cf. *Bṛhadāranyaka Upaniṣad*, IV, 5, 6); "have no ulterior purpose in thy work" (149), "work as though no one existed, no one lived, no one had ever come upon the earth" (308); "All happiness to those who have listened to this sermon. Had there been no one here I must have preached it to the poor-box" (143). "God and God's will are one, for if I am a man and if I mean to do real work entirely without or free from will . . . I should do my works in such a way that they entered not into my will. . . . I should do them simply at the will of God" (308), "Above all lay no claim to anything. Let go thyself, and let God act for thee" (308). The artist has some "inkling" (47) of God's manner of working "willingly but not by will, naturally and not by nature" (225) when he has acquired mastery and the habit (*habitus*, *śliṣṭatva*) of his work and does not hesitate but "can go ahead without a qualm, not wondering, am I right or am I doing wrong? If the painter had to plan out every brush mark before he made his first he would not paint at all" (141). Still, "Heaven does more than the carpenter who builds a house" (II, 209).

"Inspired by his art" (II, 211), "as much like his ideal as he can" (252), and "working for work's sake," sound to modern ears like art for art's sake. But "art" and "his ideal" have not here their modern sentimental connotations, they represent nothing but the artist's understanding of his theme, the work to be done (*kṛtârtha*); working for "the real intention of the work's first cause" (252) is not working for the sake of the workmanship, as the modern doctrine implies; "working for work's sake" means in freedom, without ulterior motive, easily (cf. *Bhagavad Gītā*, *passim*). To work according to the "dearest conception of his art" (97), that is with all the skill and care he can command, is merely honest, and "By honest I mean doing one's best at the moment" (II, 95), having "good grounds for thinking no one else could do the work as well" (II, 90), and standing for "perfection in temporal works" (II, 92), the "careful" being "those who let nothing hinder them in their work" (II, 90).

The first cause of the work and the good of the work to be done are one and the same, "the ultimate end (*prayojana*) of the work is ever the real intention (*artha*) of the work's first cause" (252), "when the carpenter builds a house his first intention is a roof (that is, the idea of shelter), and that is (actually) the finish of the house" (196). No man being a rational being works for no end: "The builder hewing wood and stone because he wants to build a house 'gainst summer's heat and winter's chill is thinking first and last about the house, excepting for the house he would never hew a single stone or do a hand's turn of the work" (II, 72).

The good of the work is its immediate physical good, not its edifying purpose. Actual work requires a worldly wisdom, industry, and cunning, not to be confused with vision, but matter of fact, and with due regard to the material (II, 93): for instance, "A celebrant (of the mass) over-much intent on recollection is liable to make mistakes. The best way is to try and concentrate the mind before and afterwards, but when actually saying it to do so quite straightforwardly" (II, 175). A work may be undertaken *ad majorem gloriam Dei* or to any more immediate end, but the end can only be enjoyed in the prospect or in completion of the work. In action the workman is nothing but a tool, and should use himself accordingly, concerned with the work and not with its results; he can and should be totally absorbed in the work, like the "heathen philosopher who studied mathematics . . . in pursuance of his art . . . too much absorbed to see or hear his enemy" (12). Working thus is not for the sake of or to display skill, but to serve and praise the first cause of the work, that is, the subject imaged in the artist's mind "without idea of ownership" (35). It is immaterial what the work may be, but it is essential that the artist should be wholly given to it, "it is all the same to him what he is loving" (II, 66), it is working for the love of God in any case, because the perfection of the work is "to prepare all creatures to return to God" (143) as "in their natural mode (they) are exemplified in divine essence" (253), and this will hold good even if the painter paints his own portrait, God's image in himself.[64] He is no true workman but a vainglorious showman who would astonish by his skill; "any proper man ought to be ashamed for good people to know of this in him" (II, 51); having his art which he is expected to practice, he should take his artfulness and cunning for granted. If by reason of his skill he gets a good report in the world, that is to be taken as the "gift of God" (143), not as his due who should work "as though no one existed" (308). Similarly as to wages, the workman is indeed worthy of his hire, but if he is "careful" for anything but the good of the work to be done, he is no workman but a "thrall and hireling" (149).

Working in the world "at some useful occupation" (22) is by no means any hindrance to the perfecting of the man, and though "praying is a better act than spinning" (II, 8) a man should relinquish "rapture" to engage in any activity that may be required of him by way of service (II, 14, etc.), and even that "without which I cannot get into God, is work, vocation or calling in time, which interferes not one whit with eternal salvation" (II, 93). "To be in the right state one of two things has to happen: either he must find God and learn to have him in his works, or else things and works must be abandoned altogether. But no one in this life can be without activities, human ones, and not a few at that, so man has to learn to find his God in everything" (II, 11; cf. *Bhagavad Gītā* III, 33); even for the religious "active life bridges the gaps in the life of contemplation," and, "Those who lead the contemplative life and do no outward works, are most mistaken and all on the wrong tack"; "No person can in this life reach the point at which he is excused from outward works" (425 cf. *Bhagavad Gītā*, III, 16 and 25); therefore "'work in all things' and 'fulfil thy destiny'" (165). Still more in the case of one "who knows nothing of the truth from within, if he woo it without (he) shall find it too within" (440). In any case "God's purpose in the union (*yoga*) of contemplation is fruitfulness in works" (16).

The workman is naturally happy in his work, seeing the image in his mind becoming, in the analogy of God, whose vision of all creatures is the vision of himself in himself; this pleasure taken in the sight of matter in the act of receiving form is, in the workman still at work, a form of aesthetic experience. But in what this experience essentially consists, it will be more convenient to consider from the point of view of the spectator who sees the work completed in intention or in actuality, not in the process of becoming but as it were apart from duration, for "No activity is so perfect but it hinders recollection. The hearing of the mass permits of recollection more than the saying of it does" (II, 174).

So what is aesthetic experience, or, as Eckhart calls it, recollection, contemplation, illumination (*avabhāsa*), the culminating point of vision, rapture, rest? In so far as it is accessible to man as a rumor (95) or foretaste (479), passing like a flash of lightning (255), it is the vision of the world-picture as God sees it, loving all creatures alike, not as of use, but as the image of himself in himself (360), each in its divine nature and in unity, as a conscious eye situated in a mirror (253, 384) might see all things in all their dimensions apart from time and space as the single object of its vision, not turning from one thing to another (12) but seeing without light, in a timeless image-bearing light, where "over all sensible things hangs the motionless haze of unity." That is a seeing of things in their perfection, ever verdant, unaged and unaging (36): "To have all that has being and is lustily to be desired and brings delight; to have it all at once and whole in the undivided soul and that in God, revealed in its perfection, in its flower, where it first burgeons forth in the ground of its existence . . . that is happiness" (82), a "peculiar wonder" (47), "neither in intellect nor will, . . . as happiness and not as intellection" (200), not dialectically but as if one had the knowledge and the power to gather up all time in one eternal now (81), as God enjoys himself (142, 240).

Again, it is compared to the seeing of a play, a play (*līlā*) played eternally before all creatures, where player and audience, sport and players, are the same, their nature proceeding in itself, in clear conception and delight (147, 148), or to an operation in which God and I are one, works wrought there being all living. This sharing of God's vision of himself in his "work," which in so far as we can have an "inkling" of it is what we mean by aesthetic experience, is likewise what we mean by Beauty as distinct from loveliness or liking, which have their drawbacks in their opposites. "The supremely pure splendor of the impartible essence illumines all things at once." According to Dionysius, Beauty is order, symmetry with supreme lucidity. In this sense "the Godhead is the beauty of the three Persons" (366), "beauty with which the sun is nothing to compare" (399), "each Person radiant to the rest as to itself. This illumination is the perfection of beauty." "All things tend toward their ultimate perfection" (72).

So much of pure aesthetic experience as is possible to

anyone is his guarantee of ultimate perfection and of perfect happiness. It is as artist-scholar that man prepares all things to return to God, in so far as he sees them intellectually (*parokṣāt*) and not merely sensibly (*pratyakṣeṇa*). This is from Eckhart's point of view the "meaning" of art. "That is as far as I can understand it" (282).

Chapter III

REACTIONS TO ART IN INDIA

Chapter III

REACTIONS TO ART IN INDIA

When music is too archaic or inaccessible to give us aesthetic data, more may be learned from the disposition of those who were pleased by it than from its recorded technical data.

D. F. Tovey, in Encyclopædia Britannica, s.v. *Music.*

THE purpose of the following notes is to bring together, mainly from the general, non-technical literature, a few passages in which the reaction of the public to works of art is reported, partly as a contribution to the vocabulary of criticism, but more with a view to showing how the art was actually regarded by those for whom it was made. The artist himself (*śilpin, kāraka, kavi*) is commonly described as "knowing his craft" (*śilpa-viśārada*, etc.) and as "skilful" (*kuśala*); nothing like a special sensibility or natural talent is mentioned, but we find that the moral virtues of ordinary men are expected in the artist, and for the rest he has his art which he is expected to practice. His attitude with respect to his commission is naturally expressed in *Jātaka*, II, 254, as follows, "We musicians, O king, live by the practice of our art (*sippaṁ nissāya*); for remuneration, I will play," but as numerous texts and inscriptions prove, the workman when moved by piety was ready to work gratuitously as an act of merit. In the latter case, artist and patron are one, the work being commanded by the artist's own devotional feeling. As to fame, and the purpose of the work, an illuminating couplet attributed to one of the successors of the Aṣṭacchāp of Hindī literature tells us:

Ours is true poetry, if so be it please great poets yet to come,
Otherwise, its pretext is that it is a reminder of Rādhā and
Kṛṣṇa.

The workman being a rational being, it is taken for granted that every work has a theme or subject (*vastu*, *kārya*, *kṛtârtha*, *anukārya*, *ālikhitavya*, etc.) and a corresponding utility or meaning (*artha*, *arthatā*, *prayojana*).

The general word for understanding or apprehension is *grahaṇa*, "grasping," for example, *Viṣṇudharmottara*, III, 41, 12; cf. the senses as "apprehenders" (*grahāḥ*) and ideas as "over-apprehenders," *Bṛhadāraṇyaka Upaniṣad*, III, 2, and Pali *gahaṇa* used with *sippa* to denote "learning a craft." An audience is praised as "appreciative of the merits (*guṇa-grāhiṇī*)" of a play, *Priyadarśikā*, I, 3. According to the *Abhinaya Darpaṇa*, "The audience shines like a wishing-tree, when the Vedas are its branches, *śāstras* its flowers, and learned men the bees. . . . The Seven Limbs of the audience are men of learning, poets, elders, singers, buffoons, and those versed in history and mythology," and the chief of the audience, the patron, must be a connoisseur.[65] Applause is *ukkuṭṭhi* in *Jātaka*, II, 253 and 367, more often the still current exclamation, *sādhu*, "well-done."

In the *Dūtavākya* of Bhāsa, 7, the picture (*paṭa*) of the Gambling Scene is called "admirable" (*darśanīya*, cf. modern colloquial "easy to look at"); and, after a detailed description of the subject-matter represented, Duryodhana concludes, *ibid.*, 13, "O what richness of color (*varṇâḍhyatā*)! What a presentation of the moods (*bhāvôpapannatā*)! What a skilful laying on of colors (*yuktalekhatā*)! How explicit the painting (*suvyaktam ālikhito*)! I am pleased."

As to these comments, *varṇâḍhya* is stated to be what most interests "others" (*itare janāḥ*),[66] that is, people in general, not masters (*ācārya*) or connoisseurs (*vicakṣaṇa*, *Viṣṇudharmottara*, III, 41, 11; see *JAOS.*, LII, 11, confirmed by the *Triṣaṣṭiśalākāpuruṣacaritra* passage cited below); for the expression of *bhāva* and *rasa* in painting, see *JAOS.*, LII, 15, n. 5, and Basava Raja, *Śiva-Tattva-Ratnākara*, VI, 2, 19; the exact significance of *yuktalekhatā* is less certain. Cf. the word as cited below.

Darśanīya, "worth seeing," occurs regularly in connection with pictures, sculpture, and architecture. Cf. *Cūlavaṁsa*, C, 251, *manoharaṁ dassanīyaṁ toraṇaṁ*; *ibid.*, 258, an image of the Buddha is *dassanīyaṁ . . . cārudassanaṁ*; and *ibid.*, 262, pictures are *dassaniyyâpare cārū cittakamme*; analogous is the use of *savaṇīya* (*śravaṇīya*), "worth hearing," and *savaṇīyataraṁ*, "very well worth hearing," *ibid.*, LXXXIX, 33, while the two terms are used together, *ibid.*, 35, with reference to songs and dances, which are *dassanassavaṇa-ppiyaṁ*, "pleasing to see and hear." Cf. *śrotraṁ sukhayati*, "pleases the ear," and *dṛṣṭiprītiṁ vidhatte*, "pleases the eye," with reference to natural beauties, *Priyadarśikā*, II, 4. A word very commonly applied to pictures is *manorama*, "pleasing the heart." In the *Divyâvadāna*, 361–362, Māra, at Upagupta's request, manifests himself in the form of the Buddha, with all his specific lineaments (*lakṣaṇâḍhyam*). Upagupta bows down to this representation, that is, as he explains, to him whose image it is. The aspect (*rūpa*) assumed by Māra, as an actor assumes a part, is *nayanakāntim ākṛtim*, "a representation delighting the eyes," and *nayanaśāntikaraṁ narāṇām*, "giving peace to the eye of man"; Upagupta is *abhipramudita*, *pramuditamana*, "overjoyed," *prāmodyam utpannam*, "delight overflows," and he exclaims *Aho*, *rūpa-śobhā*, *kiṁ bahunā*, "In short, what beauty of aspect!"

From a monastic point of view, usually but not exclusively Buddhist or Jaina, the arts are rejected altogether as merely a source of pleasant sensations; cf. *vāsanā* in Mahāyāna psychology as "nostalgia," but in art an indispensable innate sensibility. As a single example of the monastic attitude *Triṣaṣṭiśalākāpuruṣacaritra*, I, 1, 361, may be cited, where it is asserted that music (*saṁgīta*) in no way serves for welfare (*kuśala*), but only infatuates by giving a momentary pleasure (*muhurta-sukha*). The fact is that what Hindus mean by the "pleasure of the eyes" may or may not be a disinterested pleasure, and this has always to be determined from the context; cf. the Scholastic *id quod visum placet*.

In the *Śakuntalā* (VI, 13–14, in Kale's edition (K), *ibid.*,

VI, 15–16, in Pischel's (P), the variants in both versions being here utilized), the King, looking at his own memory picture of Śakuntalā, exclaims with reference to the subject rather than the workmanship, "O, the beauty of the painting" (*aho rūpam ālekhyasya*), and later makes a distinction between what is "right" (*sādhu*) in the work, and what is "off" or "out" (*anyathā*, not to be confused with *ardhalikhita*, "unfinished," which occurs below); still, "something of Śakuntalā's charm (*lāvaṇya*) is caught (*kiṁcid-anvita*) in the line (*rekhā*)." The Vidūṣaka finds the line (*rekhā*) full of tender sentiment (*bhāva-madhurā*, P), and the "imitation of mood in the tender passages is noteworthy" (*madhurâvasthāna-darśanīyo bhāvānupraveśaḥ*, K), alternatively "it seems to be the very rendering of reality" (*sattvânupraveśa-śa˙khaya*, P); he exclaims, "In short" (*kiṁ bahunā*, P), "she makes me want to speak to her" (*ālapana-kautūhalam me janayati*); he pretends that his eye actually stumbles (*skhalati*) over the hills and vales (*nimnônnata-pradeśeṣu*).[67] Miśrakeśī remarks on the King's skill with the "brush and in outline" (*vartikā-rekhā-nipuṇatā*), alternatively "in color and line" (*varṇa-rekhā*).

In the *Pratijñāyaugandharâyaṇa* of Bhāsa, III, 1, the court jester speaks of the skilful laying on of color (*yukta-lekhatā*) in a fresco, shown by the fact that when he rubs the painting it only grows the brighter (*ujjvalatara*).

In the *Mālavikâgnimitra*, II, 2, a lack of correspondence between the beauty of the model and that represented in the painting [68] is spoken of as *kānti-visaṁvāda*, and ascribed to imperfect concentration (*śithila-samādhi*) on the part of the painter. In the *Priyadarśikā*, III, and *Vikramôrvāśī*, II (introductory stanza), imperfections of acting are similarly ascribed to the actor's absent-mindedness (*śūnya-hṛdayatā*).

In the *Pratimānāṭaka* of Bhāsa, III, 5, Bharata, seeing the statues of his parents, whom he does not recognize, exclaims, "Ah, what sweetness in the workmanship of these stones (*aho kriyā-mādhuryaṁ pāṣāṇānām*)! Ah, what feeling (*bhāva*) is embodied in these images (*aho bhāvagatir ākṛtīnām*)!" He wonders what the figures represent, but "Anyhow, there is a great delight (*praharṣa*) in my heart," which delight is perhaps thought of not so much as aesthetic as due to a subconscious recognition of the statues as those of his parents. But *pramudaṁ prayāti*, said of the Self with respect to the pleasure felt at the spectacle of its own manifestation as the world picture (*jagaccitra*, Śaṅkarâcārya, *Svâtmanirūpaṇa*, 95), implies a delight unquestionably disinterested.

In Bhavabhūti's *Uttara-Rāma-Caritra*, I, 39, the sight of the paintings leaves a latent or persisting emotional impression (*bhāvanā*), not a mere memory, but a lingering sentiment, in Sītā's mind; this may be compared with "I still seem to hear the music as I walk," cited below, and *Śakuntalā*, V, 8 f. (Pischel), where Duḥṣanta, overhearing the singing of his Queen Haṁsavatī, soliloquizes, "What a passion-laden (*rāga-parivāhiṇī*) song! . . . Why then am I so filled with yearning by hearing such a song, as though I were divided from a loved one? Howbeit, if after seeing lovely things, or hearing sweet words, a man is saddened as well as charmed, it may be because unconsciously he remembers loves heart-felt ere birth, survivals of a former disposition (*pūrvaṁ-bhāva-sthirāṇi*)"; the stage direction follows, "He registers (*rūpayati*) perplexity occasioned by a thing forgotten."

In the case of portraits, the excellence of the likeness is naturally commented upon, for example, *Svapnavāsavadattā*, VI, 13, and *Mṛcchakaṭika*, IV, 1, the words *sadṛśī* and *susadṛśī* (not *sādṛśya*) being employed. In the *Svapnavāsavadattā*, *loc. cit.*, the Queen, looking at the picture of Vāsavadattā, is "delighted and perplexed" (*prahṛṣṭôdvignām iva*), but this is because she thinks she recognizes the person represented; it is not an aesthetic effect. In the *Mālatīmādhava*, I, 33 (9–10), the purpose of the portrait (*ālekhya-prayojana*) is said to be consolation in longing (*utkaṇṭhā-vinodana*).

The different ways in which a painting may be regarded by spectators of various classes are stated in some detail in Hemacandra's *Triṣaṣṭiśalākāpuruṣacaritra*, I, 1, 648 ff., where a painting on canvas (*paṭa*) is spread out (*vistārya*) with a practical purpose, viz. in the hope that some spectator will recognize it as a representation of the events of his own former life. Those versed in scripture (*āgamavit*) praise the representation of the Nandīśvara heavens, because "it accords with the purport of the scripture" (*āgamârthâvisaṁvādi*); the very pious (*mahāśraddha*) nod their heads and describe to one another the figures (*bimbāni*) of the saints (*jina*); those expert in the practice of the arts (*kalā-kauśala-śālin*) praise the purity of the outlines (*rekhā-śuddhi*), as they examine them again and again with sideling glances; others talk of the colors, white, black, yellow, blue, and red, that make the painting look like a brilliant sunset.

An appreciation of architectural beauty is frequently expressed in general terms; there is, for instance, a moving description of the ruined city of Poḷonnāruvā, of which the buildings "through decay and old age are like greybeards and unable to stand erect, becoming more and more bowed down from day to day," *Cūlavaṁsa*, LXXXVIII. In the same text, LXXVIII, 39, we find the phrase "creating out of brick and stone an elixir for the eyes" (*rasâyana*); cf. *netrâmṛta*, of a picture, *Avadāna Kalpalatā*, p. vii.

In the *Guttila Jātaka* (No. 243) there is a competition between two *vīṇā* players, who show their art (*sippaṁ dassesanti*) which the people see (*passanti*). At first, when both play equally well, the public is delighted (*tuṭṭho* = *tuṣṭha*).[69] The competition then becomes one not so much in musical talent as in the performance of a stunt, the victor playing on a reduced number of strings, and finally only on the body of his instrument. The public cries out against the defeated competitor, saying, "You do not know the measure (*pamāṇa* = *pramāṇa*) of your capacity."

In the *Vikramacaritra*, III, 2 (*HOS*., 26, 18 and 27, 15),[70] where there is a dancing competition between two apsarases, Vikramâditya, who knows all the arts (*sakala-kalâbhijña*) and is especially a connoisseur (*vicakṣaṇa*) of the science of the ensemble of musical arts (*saṁgīta-vidyā*), acts as judge.[71] He decides in favor of Urvaśī because she fulfils the requirements of the *Nāṭya Śāstra*, both as to her person and as to her ability; the latter is shown specifically in registering (*sūcanā*) the full meaning by means of language conveyed in bodily movements, in the accurate rhythms of the feet, in the sensitive gestures (*abhinaya*) of the hands and their agreement with the permitted variations (*tadvikalpânuvṛttau*), in the constant displacement of one mood by another in the field of representation, and in her skilful blending of the passions (*rāgabandha*). In short, "I preferred Urvaśī because I found her a danseuse of such a sort as is described in the *Nāṭya Śāstra*."

In the *Priyadarśikā*, III, where there is a play within a play, the former raises the spectator's interest to the highest degree, *adhikataraṁ kautūhalaṁ vardhayati*, which is modestly explained by the author as due to the merit of the subject. In the same act of the same work, the verb *avahṛ*, "to transport," "enrapture," is used with reference to the effects of a performance on the harp (*vīṇā*); the King, too, evokes admiration or astonishment (*vismaya*) by his performance.

In the *Mṛcchakaṭika*, III, 2–5, Cārudatta has attended a musical performance (*gāndharva*); he is reminiscent, and exclaims, "Ah, ah, well done (*sādhu*)! Master Rebhila's song was excellent (*suṣṭhu*)." Then, more technically,[72] speaking both as expert in the art and as *rasika*, "The sound was informed by the moods (*bhāva*), now passionate (*rakta*), now sweet (*madhura*), now calm (*sama*), languishing (*lalita*) and ravishing too; it seemed like the lovely voice of my own hidden love. The low progressions (*svara-saṁkrama*) seated in the vibrating strings, the crescendo (*tāra*) of the scales (*varṇa*) and modes (*mūrcchana*), and their diminuendo (*mṛdu*) in the pauses — when passion is restrained, desire repeats its languishing (*lalita*) — and though the reality was ended with the song itself, I seem to hear it as I walk." There is a similarly technical appreciation of a *vīṇā* performance in *Priyadarśikā*, III, 10.

To sum up, it will be seen that everyone is thought of as making use of the work of art in his own way, the work of visual art, no less than a word, being a *kāma-dhenu*, yielding to the spectator just what he seeks from it or is capable of understanding. Everyone is interested in the subject-matter or application of the work, as a matter of course. More specifically, we find that learned men, pundits, are concerned about the correctness of the iconography; the pious are interested in the representation of the holy themes as such; connoisseurs (*vicakṣaṇa* in the cited passages, elsewhere *rasika, pramātṛ, sahṛdaya*) are moved by the expression of *bhāva* and *rasa*, and like to express their appreciation in the technical terminology of rhetoric; masters of the art, fellow artists, regard chiefly the drawing, and technical skill in general; ordinary laymen like the bright colors, or marvel at the artist's dexterity.[73] Those who are in love are chiefly interested in portraiture reflecting all the charms (*kānti, lāvaṇya*) of the original. Rarely do we meet with any mention of originality or novelty.[74] We ought then, to appreciate Indian art from every point of view, to be equipped with learning, piety, sensibility, knowledge of technique, and simplicity: combining the qualities of the *paṇḍita*, the *bhakta*, the *rasika*, the *ācārya*, and the *alpa-buddki-jana*.

Chapter IV

AESTHETIC OF THE SUKRANĪTISĀRA

Chapter IV

AESTHETIC OF THE ŚUKRANĪTISĀRA

THE *Śukranītisāra* of Śukrâcārya is a mediaeval Indian treatise on statecraft and an encyclopaedic work on social organization considered from every point of view. In the passages dealing with the making of images are embodied some very definite statements of aesthetic principles; and as these passages have been misunderstood and mistranslated, or at least inadequately translated, it seems desirable to present a fresh and complete version. The verses translated begin with Ch. IV, Sec. 4, verse 70, the numbering being that of Vidyāsāgara's text, with those of Sarkar's translation in parentheses:[75]

"One should make use of (*yojayet*) the visual-formulae (*dhyāna*) proper to the angels (*devatā*) whose images are to be made (*ārambhya*). It is for the successful accomplishment of this practice (*yoga*) of visual-formulation (*dhyāna*) that the lineaments (*lakṣaṇa*) of images are prescribed. The human-imager (*pratimākāra*) should be expert in this visual-contemplation, since thus, and in no other way, and verily not by direct observation (*pratyakṣa*), (can the end be achieved)." 70, 71 (147–150).

"Images made of sand (*saikata*), dough (*paiṣṭa*), or painted (*lekhya*), or of stucco (*lepya*), or terracotta (*mṛṇ-*

maya), or wood (*vṛkṣa*), or stone (*pāṣāṇa*), or metal (*dhātu*) are of relative durability in the same order." 72 (151).

"Images made as directed, with all their members complete, are attractive and merit-yielding; those otherwise are destructive of life and wealth, and ever increase sorrow; one should make images of angels (*deva*), for these are productive of good, and heavenward-leading (*svargya*), but those of men or other (creatures) lead not to heaven nor are they auspicious. That image is said to be lovely (*ramya*) which is of neither more nor less than the prescribed proportions (*māna*). Images of the angels, even with lineaments (*lakṣaṇa*) imperfectly depicted, work weal to men, but never those of mortals, even though their lineaments (be accurately represented)." 73–76 (152–158).

"Images of the angels are of three sorts, pure (*sāttvika*, that is, as they are in themselves naturally), active (*rājasika*, expansive, manifesting in 'work'), and dark (*tāmasika*, effectively as if limited by the inertia of matter and engaged in actual work). Those of Viṣṇu and other angels should be employed and worshipped (*yogya pūjya*) according to the necessities of the case. A *sāttvika* image is one in a *yoga*-posture, self-supported, with hands exhibiting bounty and encouragement (*varâbhaya*), and worshipped by the premier angels and such like beings (*devendrâdi*). A *rājasika* image is one supported by a vehicle (*vāhana*), adorned with a variety of ornaments, with hands holding weapons and implements, and exhibiting bounty and encouragement. A *tāmasika* image is one of dread (*ugra*) aspect, engaged in slaying demons by means of weapons and implements, and as if eager for combat." 77–80 (159–166).

"It is prescribed that the veins of the hands and feet should not be shown, nor should the ankle-bones be seen. Those parts of images are said to be really lovely (*suśobhana*) which are neither more nor less in proportion (*māna*) than the limbs of such images as have been made by experts, and every member that is neither too thick nor too thin will be altogether pleasing (*sarvamanorama*). Although hardly one in a hundred thousand is produced that is altogether pleasing in every member, still that which accords with canonical prescription (*śāstramāna*) is alone truly lovely (*ramya*), none other, to be sure! There are some to whom that which captivates their heart (*tat lagnaṁ hṛd*) is lovely; but for those who know, that which falls short of canonical proportion (*śāstramāna*) is not beautiful." 101–106 (209–215).

"One should contrive for every member such grace (*pāṭava*) as is appropriate." 121 (256).

"In the case of painted images, or those made of stucco, sand, terracotta, or dough, an omission of lineaments (*lakṣaṇa*) will do no harm; one should beware of defects of proportion (*māna*) only in the case of images of stone or metal." 152, 153 (306, 309).

"The lineaments (*lakṣaṇa*) of images are known (*smṛta*) from the natures (*bhāva*) of the worshipped and the worshipper (*sevyasevaka*). By the power of the intension (*tapas*) of the officiant (*arcaka*) whose heart is ever set upon the Lord, the faults of an image immediately pass away." 159, 160 (320–322).

"There is no rule (*niyama*) for the thickness of the limbs of a child, they should be devised as may seem lovely." 185 (375).

"The artist (*śilpi*) should ever conceive the beauty (*vapu*) of the images (of the angels) as youthful (*taruṇa*), rarely as childlike (*bāla-sadṛśa*), never as aged (*vṛddha-sadṛśa*)." 201 (403, 404).

"The King should not set up or keep in a temple a disproportioned or broken image; worn out images of the angels, and ruined temples, are to be carefully restored." 203 (407, 408).

The following, from Section 7, refers only to figures of horses: "When a figure (*rūpa*) of a horse is to be made, the model (*bimba*) should always be in view (*vīkṣya*), and if one cannot be looked at (*adṛṣṭvā*) the figure should not be made. The artist (*śilpi*) having first (*agre*) made his visual contemplation (*dhyātvā*) on the horse and attentive to its forms (*avayavânataḥ*) should do his work, embodying all the proportions (*māna*) of horses meet for splendor and divorced from ill-omen." 73, 74 (145–147). It will be seen here, that in spite of the apparent demand for likeness to the horse in view, there is insistence on visualization and on adherence to ideal proportions.

The portions of the text omitted above provide the detailed measurements proper to the various types of beings. It will be quite evident that Śukrâcārya is propounding a purely scholastic and hieratic conception of what is lovely or beautiful, and nowhere admits the validity of individual taste. Just as Professor Masson-Oursel has pointed out,[76] "Indian art is aiming at something quite other than the copying of Nature. What we assume, quite superficially, to be the inspiration of an art for art's sake, really proceeds from a religious scholasticism that implies a traditional classification of types established by convention. If here or there a relief or painting exhibits some feature drawn from life, it is only accidentally that the artist has, in spite of himself, transcribed something from actual Nature: and this is certainly, from the indigenous point of view, the least meritorious part of his work." Those who wish to study the "development" of Indian art must emancipate themselves entirely from the innate European tendency to use a supposedly greater or less degree of the observation of Nature as a measuring rod by which to trace stylistic sequences or recognize aesthetic merit. Indian art can only be studied as showing at different times a greater or less degree of consciousness, a greater or less energy; the criteria are degrees of vitality, unity, grace, and the like, never of illusion. In India, an art of primarily representative interest, that of portraiture, was practiced mainly by amateurs, and even so required a mental visualization only less formal than that of the hieratic work; in itself the portraiture had usually an erotic purpose or content, and in any case a merely personal and temporary value, not an ultimate spiritual significance.[77]

Chapter V

PAROKṢA

Chapter V

PAROKṢA

Which things also we speak, not in the words which man's wisdom teacheth, but which the Holy Ghost teacheth.

Corinthians, I, 2, 13.

THE terms *parokṣa* and *pratyakṣa* are used in contrasted senses. The purely grammatical distinction of *parokṣa* and *pratyakṣa* need not detain us: a stanza referring to an Angel (*deva*), if voiced in the third person, is said to be *parokṣa*, "indirect," or if addressed immediately in the second person, *pratyakṣa*, "direct," *Nirukta*, VII, 1. What concerns us more is the distinction of the *parokṣa* as proper to the Angels (*adhidaivata*), who are accordingly described as *parokṣa-priya*, "fond of" the symbolic, from the *pratyakṣa* as proper to man (*mānuṣa*) as individual (*adhyātma*), who is evidently *pratyakṣa-priya*, "fond of" the obvious, though this is not explicitly stated.

In *Jaim. Up. Br.*, I, 20, *Ait. Br.*, III, 33 and VIII, 30, *Ś. Br.*, VI, 1, 1, 2 and 11 and XIV, I, 1, 13, *Bṛ. Up.*, IV, 2, 2, and *Ait. Up.*, III, 14, examples are given as follows (the *parokṣa* designations being followed in each case by the *pratyakṣa* designations printed in italics): antarikṣa, *antaryakṣa*; mānuṣa, *māduṣa*; nyagrodha, *nyagroha*; Indra, *indha*, *idandra*; Agni, *agri*; aśva, *aśru*. To these may be added from passages cited below: Ahi Budhnya, *Agni*

Gārhapatya; Soma, *nyagrodha*; and viśvajit, *vrata*. The *pratyakṣa* term stands for the *parokṣa* referent; for example, "the lotus means the Waters, this Earth is a leaf thereof," *Ś. Br.*, VII, 4, 1, 8, where lotus and leaf have physical, Waters (= Possibility) and Earth (= Ground) metaphysical, referents. Evidently it is not necessary that the *parokṣa* and *pratyakṣa* terms should be sensibly distinct; the *puṣkara* which is spoken of as the birthplace of Agni or Vasiṣṭha, and which represents the Ground of all existence, is not the *puṣkara* of the botanist, though the words are the same. The actual lotus-leaf laid down upon the Fire Altar has no necessary meaning of its own, quâ lotus-leaf; it is merely a datum with respect to which we can have only estimative or affective knowledge; it *is* the referent of *puṣkara-parṇa*, but *impersonates* the referent of the *parokṣa* term *pṛthivī*. The distinction is one of reference, which the student, guided by the context, or if necessary by the Commentator, is expected to understand;[78] and if he takes the reference literally, we say that his understanding is superficial. For the *parokṣa* and *pratyakṣa* references are not coincident: the former are names of assumed or otherwise known but not perceptible referents (cf. Śaṅkarâcārya on *Ait. Up.*, III, 14); and the latter, names of sensibly experienced referents which are, or are regarded as, merely symbols of or suitable substitutes for the aforesaid unseen referents. It follows that the reference of the *parokṣa* term is much wider than that of the *pratyakṣa* term; viz., in that of the many conceivable signs of or substitutes for the operating but unseen referent the *pratyakṣa* term specifies only one. It follows at the same time that the *parokṣa* vocabulary will be much less numerous than the *pratyakṣa*; the Angels have fewer ideas, and use less means than men.

The passage, *Ait. Up.*, III, 14, already cited, may be quoted in full. In the previous verse it is said that the Self, individually conscious in the plurality of beings, beheld the Brahman immediately, that is, recognized its manifestation in the world (cf. *Kena Up.*, 24–28), and "I have seen It (*idaṁ dadarśa*), he said." Then follows, "Therefore his name is Idaṁ-dra ('It-seeing'), Idandra indeed is his name. Him that is Idandra, the Angels speak of (lit. 'regard,' *ācakṣate*) metaphysically (*parokṣeṇa*) as Indra, for the metaphysical, indeed, is proper to the Angels." Śaṅkarâcārya comments as follows: "Because the Supreme Self saw 'This,' the immanent Brahman, face to face directly (*sākṣād aparokṣāt*), immediately (*aparokṣeṇa*) as 'This,' therefore He (the Supreme Self) is called Idandra; God (*Īśvara*) is in the world (*loke*) explicitly (*prasiddha*) by name Idandra. 'Him that is Idandra, Indra metaphysically': that is, the knowers of Brahman speak of Him thus, with metaphysical-reference (*parokṣâbhidhānena*), for practical purposes (*saṁvyavahārikârtha*) in fear of taking (*grahaṇa*) (in vain) His name who is worthy of all worship. 'The metaphysical is proper to the Angels': that is, they are wonted (*priyā*) to metaphysical (*parokṣa*) names, and it is thereby indeed that they are 'Angels.' [79] Much more so in the case of God (*Īśvara*), who is the Angel of all Angels."

Adhidaivata and *adhyātma* are contrasted in the same way as *parokṣa* and *pratyakṣa*: for example, *Kena Up.*, 29–30, with reference to the vision of Brahman. Here "with respect to the Angels" (*adhidaivata*) the vision is compared to a flash of lightning; but "with respect to the incarnate Self" (*adhyātma*) the vision is a thing which, when the Intellect (*manas*) is directed to and ponders intently on Brahman, becomes a concept (*saṁkalpa*). The *Kauṣītaki Upaniṣad*, IV, 2, gives a fuller list of correspondences, beginning with "In the Supernal Sun the Great Principle" (that is, universally, *adhidaivata*) and "In the Mirror the Counter-image" (that is, individually, *adhyātma*).

The problem presents itself both in connection with the literature, and in connection with the ritual and plastic art, the performance of the ritual, or the iconographic representation, securing "indirectly" (*parokṣeṇa*, *parokṣāt*) practical effects by setting in motion the corresponding forces. Thus the officiant "indirectly by means of Ahi Budhnya" (that is, by incantation of the verse *Ṛg Veda*, VI, 50, 14) though "directly by means of Agni Gārhapatya" (the household fire actually kindled) endows the sacrificer with fiery-energy (*tejas*), *Ait. Br.*, III, 36; the Kṣatriya who eats the shoots and fruits of the *nyagrodha* "indirectly" (*parokṣeṇa*) obtains the drinking of Soma — "he does not partake of Soma directly (*pratyakṣam*)," *ibid.*, VII, 31. Again, in the *Pañcaviṁśa Brāhmaṇa*, XXII, 9, 4 and 3, "The Viśvajit (-rite) is, indirectly, the (Mahā-)vrata; he by means thereof directly obtains food," for "What presents itself directly to men presents itself indirectly (or metaphysically) to the Angels, and what presents itself indirectly to men presents itself directly to the Angels." In this sense all the Vedic rituals are Mysterium und Mimus, Mysteries and Imitations: what anthropologists describe empirically (*pratyakṣeṇa*) as "sympathetic magic" is a metaphysical operation, an enchantment and a conjuration, not a religious, devotional service or "prayer."

In iconography, where again the terms are not of individual choice, but *śāstramāna, smṛta*, etc., we have to do with a visual language of the same kind as the verbal. The lotus of iconography is not the lotus of sensible experience; it is *parokṣa*, "not recognizable" to those who do not "understand art"; most of the accidents proper to the lotus of the botanist are omitted from the symbol, which is, moreover, of indefinite dimensions (again, "out of proportion" for those who do not "understand art," the same who say with regard to Italian primitives, "That was before they knew anything about anatomy"), *amātra*, like the *pṛthivī* that is symbolized, not like the specifically dimensioned objects (*mātrāḥ*) seen by the eye's intrinsic faculty (*cakṣuṣā*), *Maitri Up.*, VI, 6.[80] In other words, the reference of the lotus of iconography is "angelic," *adhidaivata*, that of the "lotus" of the botanist, "sensible," *pratyakṣa*.

In saying "iconography," we do not mean to distinguish iconography from art: [81] all art is "imagination," that is, a presentation of images which correspond to references originally in the mind of the artist, and not (even with the "best," or rather "worst" intentions) to any "natural," *pratyakṣa* model. For example, *Ait. Br.*, VI, 27, "It is in imitation (*anukṛti*) of the angelic (*deva*) works of art (*śilpa*) that any work of art (*śilpa*) is arrived at (*adhigam*) here;[82] for example, a clay elephant, a brazen object, a garment, a golden object, and a mule-chariot are 'works of art'; a (true) work of art is accomplished (*adhigam*) in him who comprehends this";[83] and *Śukranītisāra*, IV, 4, 70–71, where "the imager must be expert in vision (*dhyāna*), and in no other way, certainly not in the presence of a model (*pratyakṣeṇa*) can the work be accomplished." In distinguishing thus a language of symbols from a language of signs I have in mind the distinctions of symbol and sign as drawn by Jung.[84] A symbolic expression is one that is held to be the best possible formula by which allusion may be made to a relatively unknown "thing," which referent, however, is nevertheless recognized or postulated as "existing." The use of any symbol, such as the figure "*vajra*" or the word "Brahman," implies a conviction, and generally a conventional agreement resting on authority, that the relatively unknown, or it may be unknowable, referent cannot be any more clearly represented. A sign, on the other hand, is an analogous or abbreviated expression for a definitely known thing; every man knows or can be informed, by indication of an object, as to what the sign "means." Thus wings are symbols when they "mean" angelic independence of local motion, but "signs" when they designate an aviator; the cross is a symbol when used (metaphysically) to represent the structure of the Universe with respect to hierarchy and extension, but a sign when used (practically) to warn the motorist of a near-by crossroad. The use of the *words* wings or cross to designate relatively unknown, "occult," or abstract referents is symbolic, *parokṣeṇa*; their use to designate known, visible or potentially visible, concrete referents is semiotic, *pratyakṣeṇa*. Or if we use blue pigment to "represent" blue eyes or blue sky, it is as a sign; but if we make the Virgin's robe blue, then "blue" becomes the symbol of an idea, and the reference is no longer to the thing "sky" but to certain abstract qualities such as "infinity" which we have imputed to the "thing" we see overhead. In this particular case the sign and symbol are the same, viz. blue pigment, and, just as in the case of the sign or symbol *puṣkara*, lotus, the "meaning" must be understood in connection with the context. An understanding of this kind is all-important; for if we take the sign for a symbol, we shall be sentimentalizing our notion of blue eyes, and if we take the symbol for a sign, we are reducing "thought" to "recognition." In the latter case, our tacit assumption can be only that the Virgin wears the sky just as we wear our bodies, which is tantamount to speaking of the Virgin as a "personification of the sky," and to an identification of Mariolatry with the "worship of Nature." [85] The reader may suppose that such a crude mistake is impossible, as it may be impossible for him who as an inheritor of the Christian tradition knows better; nevertheless, it is this very mistake that he makes when, from a point of view supposedly "scientific" but in fact merely "profane," he speaks of Ionian philosophy as "naturalistic," or of the religion of the Vedas as a "worship of natural forces."

We are now, in the first place, led to understand how it is that in certain cases ideas, especially metaphysical or theological ideas (perhaps there are no others, "scientific" ideas being strictly speaking theological in kind) can be better communicated by visual than by verbal symbols (visual symbols will include, of course, the gestures or tones employed in ritual, as well as the surfaces of *factibilia*). The *words* "lotus," "*puṣkara*," for example, are the same however employed, *parokṣāt* or *pratyakṣeṇa*, but the lotus of iconography can scarcely be confused with the lotus of the botanist; an art in which such a confusion becomes possible is no longer art, no longer iconography, but semiotic. It is true that in the decadence of art what should be symbols are replaced by what are merely signs, a formal by an informal referendum; and in such times of decadence it is even believed that the impulses of the "Primitives" were also descriptive; it is believed, as aforesaid, that the Vedic enchantments (*mantra*) are descriptions of natural phenomena. It is just in this connection, in the second place, that we are led to understand how and why it is that "realistic" art must be regarded as "decadent," that is to say, falling short of what is proper to the dignity of man as man, to whom not merely sensible, but also intelligible worlds are accessible. Granted that by restoring to the lotus all, or all we can, of those accidents that are proper to the lotus of the botanist, we produce an object apt to deceive an animal: what we have thus done is to make it clear that our reference is, and is only, to a natural species and not to an idea; our "work of art" is no longer creative, "imitating" an exemplary form,[86] but merely a succedaneum, more or less apt to titillate the senses. If bees have been deceived by painted flowers, why was not honey also provided? The more an image is "true to nature," the more it lies. It lies in both senses, *parokṣa* and *pratyakṣa*: the portrait of the artist's wife posing as the Mother of God is untrue in its implication of likeness (the being of the Mother of God is not in the human mode), and on the other hand, the portrait of the artist's wife as such is untrue with respect to human affectibility, in that it cannot take the place of living flesh ("The eye in itself is a better thing than the eye as painted on the wall," Eckhart). Hence the *Śukranītisāra*, IV, 4, 76, speaks of portraiture as "unheavenly," *asvargya*, and the doctors of Islam disparage representative art because it simulates the work of the Supreme Artist, and is yet devoid of life.

Innumerable examples of the correspondence between what is known to the Angels in one way, to man in another could, of course, be accumulated from the Vedic literature. That these correspondences are thought of as real and necessary implies the notion of the analogical relationship of macrocosm and microcosm, such as is most explicitly asserted in *Ait. Br.*, VIII, 2, where each of the two worlds "this" and "that" is *anurūpam*, "in the image of" the other. And if in fact the word *parokṣa* is not found in the

Ṛg Veda, the notion of an angelic language distinct from that of man is there very clearly expressed in other ways. It will suffice to cite I, 164, 10, 37 and 45: "There on the pitch of heaven (*dyu*) they chant (*mantṛ*) a Wisdom (*vāc*) that is all-knowing (*viśvā-vid*) but not-all-animating (*aviś-vaminva*, perhaps 'all-disposing')"; that is, in accord with Sāyaṇa, the Angels communicate with each other in a hidden (*gupta*) language, which embraces all things but does not extend to, or is not understood by, all (*na sarva-vyāpakam*). Again, "When the First-born of the Law (sc. Agni, or the Sun) approached me, then got I a share of that Wisdom." What is meant by "a" share appears in the verse 45, "Wisdom (*vāc*) has been measured out in four degrees (*pada*), the comprehending Brahmaṇa knows them: three kept close hid (*guhā nihitā*) cause no motion (*na iṅgayanti* glossed by Sāyaṇa *na ceṣṭante*, 'do not strive,' or 'make no gesture'); men speak only the fourth degree of Wisdom." The *mantra* is quoted in *Jaim. Up. Br.*, I, 7, where the three degrees are said to be the (three) Worlds; the notion being evidently the same as that of *Maitri Up.*, VI, 6, where *Prajāpati* "utters" the Three Worlds which are his cosmic (*lokavat*) manifestation (*tanū* = *rūpa*), these "utterances" (*vyāhṛtiḥ*, viz. *Bhūr*, *Bhuvas*, *Svar* = Dante's *infima parta*, *mezza*, and *cima del mondo*) being the "names" or "forms" (*nāma*) of the Worlds. The triplicity of the utterance corresponds to the triunity of the speaker, these Worlds being the spheres of Śiva, Brahmā, and Viṣṇu, or Agni, Vāyu (or Indra) and Āditya.[87] The three utterances are simple, but exemplary; they confess all things, but do not specify them. These three parts of Wisdom (or "Speech") are said to be "hidden" and to "make no gesture," because, although the Worlds are moved *by* them, *they* do not move, but are only "thought" and immanent: "He thinks them, and behold they are" (Eckhart).[88] It is Man who by giving names to things (*nāma-dheya*, *Ṛg Veda*, X, 71, 1) contracts and identifies (*vi-dhā*, *vyākṛ*, *vi-kalp*) things into variety in time and space, and so completes the creation in its kinds, as is also to be understood in Genesis, II, 19–20. By "Man," not you and I individually, but Universal Man as Seer (*ṛṣi*) or Poetic Genius (*kavi*) is to be understood. No doctrine of solipsism is involved.

That "men speak only the fourth degree of Wisdom" corresponds to *Ṛg Veda*, X, 90, 4, "Only one fourth of Him is born here," that is to say, in time and space. *Maitri Up.*, VII, 11 (8), and *Māṇḍūkya Up.* make it clear that this one fourth corresponds to the three states (*āvasatha*) or levels (*sthāna*) of being, known as "Waking," "Dreaming," and "Deep Sleep," while the aforesaid three fourths correspond to that inscrutable (*anirukta*, *avācya*, etc.) level of "Non-duality" (of manifestation and non-manifestation, Apara- and Para-Brahman) which is spoken of as "Fourth" with respect to the three states of "Waking," "Dreaming" and "Deep Sleep."

How then can we determine the *parokṣa* level of reference more exactly? The "three quarters of Him," the Fourth state, Parabrahman, Eckhart's "Godhead," is excluded from the problem in that understanding there is neither thought nor spoken; on the other hand, the *parokṣa* language is certainly not inaccessible to human beings, since the Vedic mantras and other traditional scriptures spoken in this language are accessible to any student. Our enquiry must start from the indications given that the level of reference is *adhidaivata*, "angelic," as distinguished from *adhyātma* or *mānuṣa*, "having reference to oneself," and "human" or "mortal." What is "angelic," and what "human"? In terms of Scholastic philosophy, "purely intelligible," and "rational," respectively, nor could any better answers be given in as brief a form. Angels, however, are of many hierarchies and orders: God himself is Mahādeva, the Supreme Angel, or Devadevānām-Devâtideva, Angel of the Angels (cf. "Rex angelorum"), and on the other hand, even the powers of the individual soul may be spoken of as *devāḥ*. In any case, "The kingdom of heaven is within you," "All deities reside in the human breast" (Blake), where "within you" is *antarbhūtasya khe*, and "breast" is *hṛdaya*; cf. *Jaim. Up. Br.*, I, 14, *mayy etāḥ sarvā devatā . . . bhavanti*, "all these Angels are in me." "Human," on the other hand, as is proved by the equivalence *adhyātma* = *mānuṣa*, and by the correlation of "Human" understanding with the three states of "Waking," "Dreaming," and "Deep Sleep" (and not merely with the first of these), has by no means merely a "corporeal" connotation but one involving all extensions and transpositions of individuality. The state of Deep Sleep, in particular, though super-individual, is still "human" in that a return from this condition to that of corporeality is always possible, by way of *avataraṇa*, "special incarnation," or in the return from *samādhi* to worldly consciousness. It is perfectly clear therefore that the *parokṣa* and *pratyakṣa* understandings are not divided by an impassable wall (we have already seen that "this" and "that" are in the image of one another), but in their degrees represent a hierarchy of types of consciousness extending from animal to deity, and according to which one and the same individual may function upon different occasions. We can only determine the "level of reference" absolutely if we confine our attention to the limiting conditions.

If we ask in this sense at what level of awareness the metaphysical understanding (*parokṣa jñāna*) is all-sufficient, and specific reference superfluous, the answer can be found in *Ṛg Veda* I, 164, 10, *divo pṛṣṭhe*, "on the back (that is, top) of heaven," for it is there that the Angels communicate with one another in a purely *parokṣa* fashion, such speaking being called a chanting (*mantrayante*, "they incant"), and there that the "utterance" of the "Angel of all the Angels" is primordially "heard." That is in the Paradise of Brahmā as described in *Kauṣītaki Up.*, I, 3 ff., beyond the Solar "gateway of the worlds," kept by Agni, the Angel of the Flaming Sword. That is in human (*mānuṣa*) language called "Deep Sleep," but angelically speaking, "Pure Intelligence (*prajñā*)"; "it is a unified and mere understanding (*ekībhūtaḥ prajñāna-ghana*)," [89] *Māṇḍūkya Up.*, 5, and characterized by "the cessation of the consciousness of particulars," *Sar-*

vopaniṣatsāra, 7. The Buddhist equivalents are Sukhāvatī, Sambhogakāya; Christian, the Empyrean or Motionless Heaven, there is the "peace that passeth understanding," "Come unto Me, and I will give you rest," that rest being precisely our "Deep Sleep." Needless to say that rest and sleep which can only be represented to the "Waking" level of reference as an idling and unconsciousness are on the level of "Deep Sleep" a preëminent and creative activity. "Dreaming" and "Deep Sleep" are not places, but conditions of being, "close kept in the empty chamber of the heart," *guhā nihitam*, *antarbhūtasya khe*, *antarhṛdayâkāśe*. There within us are the angelic "levels of purely intelligible reference."

The text of *Māṇḍūkya Up.*, 5, continues, *ānanda-mayo hy ānanda-bhuk*, "in the modality of Ecstasy, enjoying Love." Here *ānanda* represents the transformation (*parāvṛtti*)[90] of carnal love, just as *prajñā* the transformation of carnal understanding; the Love is in Eckhart's sense, "We desire a thing while as yet we do not possess it. When we have it, we love it, desire then falling away." Heavenly being is thus at once intellectual and ecstatic. With this conception, and in connection with what has already been said with respect to levels of reference in art, may be cited the definition of aesthetic experience (*rasâsvādana*, "tasting of the tincture") in the *Sāhitya Darpaṇa*, III, 2–4, as *ānanda-cin-maya*, "in the mode of ecstasy and intellect," *lokôttara-camatkāra-prāṇaḥ*, "whereof the life is a supersensual flash," *vedyântara-sparśa-śūnyaḥ*, "without contact of aught else known," *brahmâsvāda-sahôdaraḥ*, "very twin of the tasting of Brahman," and *sacetasām anubhavaḥ pramāṇaṁ tatra kevalam*, "whereof the only evidence is that of intellectual men."

We have not thus far taken into consideration that *pratyakṣa* (= *aparokṣa*, *sâkṣāt*) is of two very different kinds, with respect to which *parokṣa* occupies a middle place. The *pratyakṣa* so far considered is *saṁvyavahārika*, "worldly," or "practical," proper to the human mode of being. But there is also a *paramârthika-pratyakṣa* (= *aparokṣa-sâkṣāt*) which transcends even angelic modes of understanding and communication. In one way or another, universally or specifically, "the Self (*ātman*) knows everything. But where understanding (*vijñāna*) is without duality (*advaita*), footloose of cause, effect, and operation, wordless, incomparable, and inexplicable . . . what is that? That does not belong to speech (*tad avācyam*)," *Maitri Up.*, VI, 7. As it is said elsewhere, "This Brahman is silence." Knowledge in this sense, neither of the senses nor the intellect, is spoken of as evident (*pratyakṣa*, *sâkṣāt*) only analogically, with respect to its immediacy. It is *aparokṣa* in both senses, as "self-evident," and "non-symbolic." That which is alien to all speech (*avācya*), and transmundane (*avyavahārika*), is alien equally to *saṁvyavahārika-pratyakṣa* and to *parokṣa* understanding, both of which are in the domain of *avidyā*, where things are spoken of in likenesses. There, there are neither signs nor symbols, reference nor referent; "it" can only be realized immediately, beyond all levels of reference.

It may be observed that with respect to all three kinds of reference, human, angelic, and transcendental, the eye (*akṣa, cakṣu*) is used as the symbol of perception by the senses (actually or analogically), the ear with respect to intellectual reference, thought of as "audition" rather than as hearing, "by the ear" (*śrotreṇa*) in this sense being equivalent to *parokṣa*, "not by the eye," where "eye" stands for the external senses. In the terminology under discussion, three different "eyes" are in question, viz. the carnal eye or eye's intrinsic faculty (*māṁsa-cakṣu*), the angelic eye (*divya-cakṣu*), and the eye of wisdom (*jñāna-cakṣu*, etc.). "Knowledge" accessible to the first two of these is a merely relative or false knowledge (*avidyā*); only that of the last is a true knowledge (*vidyā*) in undifferentiated sameness. Angelic understanding, in that it embodies elements of multiplicity, remains "relative" (*avidyā*), though at its highest level, being in unity, it is virtually absolute (*vidyā*).

How then should the terms *parokṣa* and *pratyakṣa* be translated? Translators of the passages cited above have rendered *parokṣa* as follows:[91] "mystic" or "esoteric" (Eggeling), "cryptic" (Hume and Caland), "mysterious" (Max Müller and Keith), "incognito" (S. Sitaram Sastri), "not recognizable," "occult" (Oertel), "indirect" (Sarup). Le P. Dandoy renders "médiat," in contrast to (*paramârthika-*)*pratyakṣa*, "immédiat."[92] For the paired terms, *parokṣa* and (*vyavahārika-*)*pratyakṣa* we have already employed or now suggest: angelic, *human*; indirect, *direct*; symbolic, *semiotic*; noumenal, *phenomenal*; universal, *par-*

ticular; theoretical, *practical*; abstract, *concrete*; intelligible, *sensible*; metaphorical, *literal*.

Amongst these terms, "indirect" and "direct" are obviously satisfactory with respect to the purely grammatical definitions, and in the other connection "direct" has the further advantage of corresponding to both senses of *pratyakṣa*. "Immediate" is evidently satisfactory for *paramârthika-pratyakṣa*, but "mediate" evidently unsatisfactory for *parokṣa*, inasmuch as the Angels use less and not more means than men; *saṁvyavahārika-pratyakṣa* is not "immediate" in the technical sense of this word, but merely "*sensibly perceptible*," or rather "*having a perceptible referent*." For *parokṣa*, terms implying incomprehensibility are certainly to be avoided,[93] inasmuch as *parokṣa* is precisely the "intelligible" as contrasted with the "sensible"; "obscure" and "mysterious" are thus excluded, but "secret" or "hidden" (Sāyaṇa's "*gupta*") are not incorrect.[94] "Mystic" is unfortunate as having a connotation distinct from, and "inferior" to, that of "metaphysical," and also because "mystic" is often confused with "mysterious." "Esoteric," in relation to "exoteric," represents a kind of distinction hardly proper to metaphysics. "Occult" is excellent, if it can be made evident that the meanings now associated with "occultism" are excluded. "Angelic" in relation to "human" is correct in reference, but not a translation. We suggest as the most desirable renderings, for (*vyavahārika-*) *pratyakṣa*, either "direct," "evident," "obvious," or "semiotic"; for *parokṣa*, either "indirect," "metaphysical," "occult," "universal," "abstract," or "symbolic"; for *paramârthika-pratyakṣa* (= *aparokṣa, sâkṣāt*), "immediate."

One further point: in the often recurring expression *parokṣa-priyā iva devāḥ*, "*priyā*" must not be rendered "are fond of," because the *parokṣa* understanding is an angelic property, depending not on choice but on nature; it is no doubt true that the Angels "love what is their own" (that is, would not be other than they are), but we cannot imply that this "love" is an "affection" — it is their being, not an accident of being;[95] cf. *Maitri Up.*, VI, 34, "What is one's thought, that he becomes," and similarly *Dhammapada*, I, 1, 2. The last consideration reminds us that in so far as man employs and understands angelic means of communication, the "language of birds," he is of the angelic kind ("Intellect is the swiftest of birds," *mano javiṣṭhaṁ patayatsu antaḥ*, *Ṛg Veda*, VI, 9, 5); in so far as his communications and understanding are limited to "matters of fact," he is not merely "a little" but a great deal "lower than the Angels."

Chapter VI

ĀBHĀSA

Chapter VI

ĀBHĀSA

ĀBHĀSA, literally "shining back," "reflection," "semblance," is predicated of the individual self (*jīva*) with respect to Brahman (*Vedânta Sūtra*, II, 3, 50, Śaṅkarâcārya explaining *ābhāsa* as "counter-image," or "reflection," *pratibimba*). In theistic texts, such as those of northern Śaivism, *ābhāsa* implies the world conceived as a theophany. The true Self "counter-sees itself" reflected in the possibilities of being (*Pañcaviṁśa Brāhmaṇa*, VII, 8, 1), as the world-picture (*jagac-citra*) painted by the Self on the canvas of the Self (Śaṅkarâcārya).[96] "He illumines (*bhāsayati*) these worlds. . . . He gladdens (*rañjayati*, 'colors') these worlds" (*Maitri Upaniṣad*, VI, 7); that is, "God made man in His own image"; *bhāsa* is Eckhart's "image-bearing light"; cf. *citra-bhāsa*, *Ṛg Veda*, VI, 10, 3, *sarūpa jyoti*, *ibid.*, X, 55, 3, *bhā-rūpa*, *Maitri Upaniṣad*, VI, 4. *Ābhāsa*, then, and *citra*, "art," are fundamentally "image," owing such reality as may be theirs to That whose image they reflect.

In Śilpa usage, as I have shown in *JAOS.*, XLVIII, 251, *ābhāsa* means "painting," and not some mysterious and otherwise unknown material, as suggested by Acharya,

Dictionary of Hindu Architecture, p. 63, and *Mānasāra*, p. 71. I now offer in support of the same view the translation of a text not cited by Acharya, viz. the *Kāśyapaśilpa*, Ch. L, *Pratimā-lakṣaṇa*, vv. 1–7 (Ānandâśrāma Series, No. 95, p. 167):

1. Hearken with singly-directed mind to the exposition of the characteristics of images, the immovable, the movable, and those both movable and immovable, which form a class of three.[97]

2. Those made of terracotta (*mṛnmaya*) or laterite (*śārkara*), of stucco (*sauyaja*), or painted (read *ālekhyaṁ*, cf. *lekhyaṁ* in *Śukranītisāra*, IV, 4, 70), are the immovable; those made of stone, wood, mineral (*dhātu*, possibly jade), or gem,

3. Are both immovable and movable; those of metal (*loha*) are the immovable. (Further) *ardha-citra*, *citra*, and *citrâbhāsa* form a class of three,

4. (of which) *ardha-citra* ('half-representation,' high relief) is an image in which half the body is not seen (read *ardhângadarśanam*), *citra* (full round representation) is when the image is visible all round (*sarvâyavasaṁdṛṣṭaṁ*),[98]

5. (And) *ābhāsa* (painting) is said with respect to an image on a canvas or wall (made to appear as if) in relief (*nimnônnate paṭe bhittau*). (Further), *ardha-citra* is done in plaster (*sudhā*), being half in the power of the other full-round representation (*citra*),

6. (And) *ābhāsa* (painting) is to be done with mineral colors (*dhātu*),[99] and so also *citrârdha* (= *ardha-citra*). But

paintings (*citrâbhāsa*) of the Angels are (also) of three kinds, best, middling, and good,

7. (For example), a base (*pīṭha*) of (plain) brick is good, a painted one (*ābhāsaka*) is better, and one of painted terracotta relief (*ābhāsârdham mṛnmayaṁ*) is best.

Another source not cited by Acharya is the *Śilparatna*, XLVI, 1–11; here *citra*, *ardha-citra*, and *citrâbhāsa* are similarly distinguished, the first being *sarvâṅga-dṛśyakaraṇaṁ*, "having all its parts visible," the second *bhittyādau lagna-bhāvenâpy-ardhaṁ*, "when half of its being is attached to a wall or the like surface," and the third is referred to as a *vilekhanaṁ*, "painting," and further, as *lekhyaṁ* . . . *nānā-varṇânvitaṁ*, "painted with the use of many colors." It is also stated that *citra* and *citrârdha* may be done in clay or plaster, wood, stone, or metal.

Ābhāsa is used in Śilpa texts also in another sense,[100] with reference to the unit of measurement proper to be employed in various kinds of buildings, the four different units specified being *jāti*, the full cubit (*hasta*), *chanda*, three-quarter cubit, *vikalpa* (not defined), and *ābhāsa*, half cubit. These units are employed respectively in building for Gods and Brahmans, Kṣatriyas, Vaiśyas, and Śūdras. It is therefore clear that *ābhāsa* represents here the least in a series of modifications or transformations of a whole unit. This meaning is quite consistent with that of *ābhāsa*, "painting," regarded as a modification of *citra*, "full-round representation," that of *rasâbhāsa*, "semblance of flavor" in Alaṁkāra terminology, *vastrâbhāsa*, "semblance of clothes" in a painting (*Pañcadaśī*, VI, 6), *cid-ābhāsa*, "reflection of absolute intelligence," *ibid.*, 7, and that of *ābhāsa* as "theophany."

Ābhāsa-gata occurs in Vasubandhu, *Abhidharmakośa*, V, 34 (Poussin, p. 72), with the related meaning "in the field of objective experience," *ābhāsa* being equivalent to *viṣaya-rūpatā*, "sensible objectivity," and *ābhāsa-gata* to *dṛśya*, "empirically perceptible." Dignāga uses *ava-bhāsate* with reference to the seemingly objective character of an intellectual image (*antarjñeya-rūpa*); *ava-bhāsa* can also be used for "illumination" as a spiritual experience. *Bhāvâbhāsa* is "semblance of existence." The opposite of *ābhāsa* is *nir-ābhāsa* or *an-ābhāsa*, "imageless."[101]

The word *ābhāsa* as "painting" involves some interesting considerations bearing on the psychological conception of the relation of painting to sculpture and relief, and on the idea of the third dimension in painting. Verse 5b, literally translated above, implies, as does also the very word *citrâbhāsa*, literally "the shining forth or semblance of *citra*," that painting is thought of as a constricted *mode* of sculpture; relief, which may also be colored, logically occupying an intermediate place. The view that painting, although actually applied to plane surfaces, was nevertheless conventionally regarded as a kind of solid representation can be supported by additional literary evidences. For example, in Vinaya, IV, 61, a monk "raises" (*vuṭṭhāpeti*) a picture (*cittam*) on a cloth; and in *Saṁyutta Nikāya*, Comm., II, 5, a painter "raises up" (*samuṭṭhāpeti*) a shape (*rūpam*) on a wall surface by means of his brushes and colors. In the *Mahāyāna Sūtrâlaṁkāra* of Asaṅga, XIII, 17, we have *citre . . . natônnataṁ nâsti ca, dṛśyate atha ca,* "there is no actual relief in a painting, and yet we see it there," and similarly in the *Laṅkâvatāra Sūtra*, Nanjio's ed., p. 91, a painted surface (*citrakṛta-pradeśa*) is said to be seen in relief (*nimnônnata*) though actually flat (*animnônnata*). In more than one place we have the metaphor of the eyes stumbling (*skhalati*) over the elevations and depressions (*nimnônnata*) represented in a picture, these hills and vales being either those of the luxuriant forms of women, or those of the landscape background (*Śakuntalā*, VI, 13–14, and perhaps *Triṣaṣṭiśalākāpuruṣacaritra*, I, 1, 360). And in verse 5a, translated above, *nimnônnate* in agreement with *paṭe* and *bhittau* is especially noteworthy, the canvas or wall being spoken of as "in relief," though it is quite certain that a plane painted surface is all that is referred to.

Natônnata and *nimnônnata* thus provide us with exact terms for the relievo, plastic modelling, or modelling in abstract light [102] which is actually seen in the paintings of Ajaṇṭā, while for the process of "shading" by which the relief effect was created and sense of volume conveyed, we have the term *vartanā*, and corresponding Pali *vattana* and *ujjotana*, "shading" and "adding high lights," in a passage of the *Atthasālinī*.[103] Such relievo must not, of course, be confused with anything of the nature of "effect of light," chiaroscuro, *chāyâtapa*,[104] "shade and shine." Relievo and chiaroscuro are indeed not merely independent, but actually contradictory notions, as was realized in Europe even as late as the time of Leonardo, who, though as a naturalist he had long studied the effects produced by direct sunlight and cast shadows, rightly maintained that these effects destroyed the representation of true relief or volume.

The question of relief involves to some degree that of perspective. Recent discussions of the problems of spatial representation in Far Eastern and Indian art [105] convey the impression that the authors are devoting much labor to what is really a rather artificial problem, posed for them by the unfamiliarity of the arts in question, this unfamiliarity persisting despite their good knowledge of the arts themselves as they exist in countless extant and accessible examples. It is difficult to believe that problems of spatial representation were ever in Asia attacked as such, in the sense that they were wrestled with in Quattrocento Italy, that is to say from a scientific and visualistic rather than an aesthetic point of view. It is surely impossible to believe that there was ever a time when art was unintelligible to those for whom it was made, for in this case it must have been unintelligible also to those who made it — the "artist" not being, as at the present day he is, an isolated and peculiar person. To suppose that art was unintelligible, and that artists, in the goodness of their hearts, were trying to make it comprehensible either to themselves or others, is as if to suppose that speakers made sounds with a view to the subsequent formation of a valid means of communication, or that carpenters began to build houses with a view to the appearance of architecture, whereas in fact speech is always adequate to the thing to be expressed, and there can no more be a progress in art than in metaphysics, but only a varying development of different aspects.

All men, and even animals, are aware that objects stand apart from each other in space, up and down, sideways, and backwards; and if animals have not a word for "three dimensions," they still know how to move in different directions, and have a sense of far and near. Space, then, has to be taken for granted as a primary datum of intelligence, and it is obvious that as soon as it became possible to make intelligible representations of objects, it must have been taken for granted by those who understood them that these were representations of objects existing in space. The question of perspective thus becomes a purely historical and descriptive problem; the definition of perspective reduces itself to "means employed to indicate the existence or distribution of objects in space." From the aesthetic point of view, no one variety of perspective can be regarded as superior to any other, and though we naturally prefer that kind of perspective which best corresponds to our own habits of vision and therefore requires least efiort of comprehension, all that is really required is intelligibility. It is in fact perfectly possible to learn to read the perspective of an unfamiliar art as fluently as we read that of our own times, and in the same way without being actively conscious of the use of any particular mode of perspective. The question of optical plausibility therefore does not arise, since it always inheres in the kind of perspective to which we are or have become accustomed; if by optical plausibility we mean anything more than this, it can only be in connection with a naïvely illusionistic view of art, as if we wished to paint a picture of the master that should be recognized by the dog.

A discussion of the history of perspective in India, and of the related problem of continuous representation, would take us too far afield; but it may be remarked that while the necessities of iconography, so far as *sāttvika* representations are involved, determine the predominance of frontality at all times, there is a representation of free movement from the earliest times, at Mohenjodaro, in Maurya terracottas, and even at Bhārhut.[106] If we consider literary sources from the Gupta period onward we find a tabulated scheme of positions (*sthāna*) ranging from the frontal (*ṛju*) through stages of *profil perdu* to strict profile (*bhitti-gata*, "gone into the wall") and mixed views, as well as a series of terms denoting various degrees of bending and torsion of the body.[107] The various positions are defined by reference to actually or ideally suspended threads, in terms of the distance between given points on the body and the threads themselves, and also in terms of *kṣaya-vṛddhi*, "loss and gain," that is effectively foreshortening, the parts which in a given position are not seen being described as *chāyā-gata*, "gone into shadow." All these are matters belonging to the history of technique rather than that of principle.

As to the development, it may be added that while the

early sculpture in the round exhibits the strongest possible feeling for plastic volume, the early reliefs (*ardha-citra*) approximate rather to painting (*citrâbhāsa*) than to solid sculpture (*citra*), being, for example at Bhārhut, closely compressed between the two planes of the wrought surface, though there are already exceptions to this at Bhājā.[108] Then at Sāñcī the relief is heightened, and the effect moves in the opposite direction from that of painting to that of round sculpture; this tendency continues throughout the Kuṣāna and later Āndhra periods, and reaches its fullest development in the Gupta period, and subsequently persists, notwithstanding that the intrinsic quality of the volume represented is no longer the same. Needless to say, early Chinese "relief" is still more like painting than is early Indian, being in fact only an engraving on stone, employing perspective methods rather difficult to grasp, but in any case not in the nature of foreshortening as in sculpture; later, the raising of the relief in Chinese stone sculpture is a reflection of Indian methods.

But the earliest Indian relief, notwithstanding its compression, has always the intention of solidity, and the earliest Indian painting by its emphatic modelling demonstrates its close relation to the contemporary sculpture in the round, with its impressive volume and mass. A like volume found expression in the reliefs only gradually, which might perhaps be thought of as indicating a later origin of relief technique, and the historical precedence of full-round sculpture and painting. However this may be, in mediaeval times the two tendencies crossed as it were in opposite directions, the one maintaining in fact a high relief, the other representing a flattening of the mental image. When sculpture gradually lost its sense of plastic volume, painting was also actually flattened out; for example, the phrase *nimnônnata-paṭa* could hardly be applied to any painting of the Gujarātī or Rajput schools, where only vestiges of the old plastic shading survive. The flattening of the visual concept must be related to a corresponding psychological modification, and certainly not to any change in technical procedure undertaken for its own sake; for thought precedes stylistic expression in the work, and to seek for the causes of changes in the changes themselves would be a *reductio ad absurdum* of history.[109]

Psychological changes, manifested in attenuation of form, can only be thought of as representing a slackening of energy, a looser concentration, *śithila-samādhi*. When one considers the impressive volumes of the earlier art, in which the form is as it were pressed outward from within by an indomitable will, one thinks also of those numerous passages in literature where the hero is said to swell with anger, or of women's bodies that expand in adolescence or in passion, or of those pregnant trees whose pent-up flowering must be released by the touch of a lovely foot. With the passing of time all these energies were and must have been brought under greater control, softened and refined in expression, the will no longer asserting, but now rather realizing itself in an active quiescence. We feel this already in the relative serenity of Gupta sculpture and the sophisticated poesy of the classical drama; we could not imagine in the twelfth century such heroic forms as those of the figures of donors at Kārlī, or that of Friar Bala's "Bodhisattva" at Sārnāth. The impulsive and ruthless heroism of the past survives only in the tradition of Rajput chivalry. In general, the tendency is toward a more purely intellectual conception of experience. It is perhaps worth noting that a like development was also taking place in contemporary mediaeval Europe, as will be apparent if for example we compare St Thomas with Śaṅkarâcārya; in neither case can it be said that any outward disorder could interfere with the supremacy of intellect.

It would be too easy to exaggerate the nature of the change, and very much mistaken to evaluate it only in terms of decadence. Stylistic sequences in thought and art are not in themselves pure loss or pure gain, decadence or progress, but necessary and therefore acceptable developments of special aspects. When the will has been in some measure appeased, the intellect can the better exercise its power. If this change of direction at first involves a loss of animal perfection (immediacy of action), it is nevertheless a becoming toward a higher spontaneity, in which the unity of the inner and outer life is to be restored, and there are even moments at the height of a development and in the lives of individuals when the balance seems to be restored and art transcends style. Apart from these questions of perfection, it might well be argued that the flattening out of art, implying as it does a more conventional symbolism than even that of modelling in abstract light, reflects a more intellectual mode of understanding, which does not require even a suggestion of modelling as an aid to reproduction; as in the case of the angels who have fewer ideas and use less means than men.

In any case, one could not, if one would wish to, turn back the movement of time. To be other than we are would be for us the same as not to be; to wish that the art of any period had been other than it was is the same as to wish that it had never been. Every style is complete in itself, and to be justified accordingly, not to be judged by the standards of a former or any other age.

> With one voice which is wondrous
> He giveth utterance to thoughts innumerable,
> That are received by audiences of all sorts,
> Each understanding them in his own way. [110]

Chapter VII

THE ORIGIN AND USE OF IMAGES IN INDIA

Chapter VII

THE ORIGIN AND USE OF IMAGES IN INDIA

It may be said that images are to the Hindu worshipper what diagrams are to the geometrician.

Rao, *Elements of Hindu Iconography*, II, 28.

FEW of those who condemn idolatry, or make its suppression a purpose of missionary activity, have ever seriously envisaged the actual use of images, in historical or psychological perspective, or surmised a possible significance in the fact that the vast majority of men of all races, and in all ages, including the present, Protestants, Hebrews, and Musalmans being the chief exceptions, have made use of more or less anthropomorphic images as aids to devotion. For these reasons it may be not without value to offer an account of the use of images in India, as far as possible in terms of thought natural to those who actually make use of such images. This may at least conduce to a realization of the truth enunciated by an incarnate Indian deity, Kṛṣṇa, that "the path men take from every side is Mine."

In explaining the use of images in India, where the method is regarded as edifying, it should not be inferred that Hindus or Buddhists are to be represented *en masse* as less superstitious than other peoples. We meet with all kinds of stories about images that speak, or bow, or weep;

images receive material offerings and services, which they are said to "enjoy"; we know that the real presence of the deity is invited in them for the purpose of receiving worship; on the completion of an image, its eyes are "opened" by a special and elaborate ceremony.[111] Thus, it is clearly indicated that the image is to be regarded as if animated by the deity.[112]

Obviously, however, there is nothing peculiarly Indian here. Similar miracles have been reported of Christian images; even the Christian church, like an Indian temple, is a house dwelt in by God in a special sense, yet it is not regarded as his prison, nor do its walls confine his omnipresence, whether in India or in Europe.

Further, superstition, or realism, is inseparable from human nature, and it would be easy to show that this is always and everywhere the case. The mere existence of science does not defend us from it; the majority will always conceive of atoms and electrons as real things, which would be tangible if they were not so small, and will always believe that tangibility is a proof of existence; and are fully convinced that a being, originating at a given moment of time, may yet, as that same being, survive eternally in time. He who believes that phenomena of necessity stand for solid existing actualities, or that there can exist any empirical consciousness or individuality without a material (substantial) basis, or that anything that has come into being can endure as such forever, is an idolater, a fetishist. Even if we should accept the popular Western view of Hinduism as a polytheistic system, it could not be maintained that the Indian icon is an any sense a fetish. As pointed out by Guénon, "Dans l'Inde, en particulier, une image symbolique representant l'un ou l'autre des 'attributs divins,' et qui est appelée *pratīka*, n'est point une 'idole,' car elle n'a jamais été prise pour autre chose que ce qu'elle est réellement, un support de méditation et un moyen auxiliaire de realization" (*Introduction à l'étude des doctrines hindoues*, p. 209). A good illustration of this is to be found in the *Divyâvadāna*, Ch. XXVI, where Upagupta compels Māra, who as a *yakṣa* has the power of assuming shapes at will, to exhibit himself in the shape of the Buddha. Upagupta bows down, and Māra, shocked at this apparent worship of himself, protests. Upagupta explains that he is not worshipping Māra, but the person represented—"just as people venerating earthen images of the undying angels, do not revere the clay as such, but the immortals represented therein."[113] Here we have the case of an individual who has passed beyond individuality, but is yet represented according to human needs by an image. The principle is even clearer in the case of the images of the angels; the image *per se* is neither God nor any angel, but merely an aspect or hypostasis (*avasthā*) of God, who is in the last analysis without likeness (*amūrta*), not determined by form (*arūpa*), trans-form (*para-rūpa*). His various forms or emanations are conceived by a process of symbolic filiation. To conceive of Hinduism as a polytheistic system is in itself a naïveté of which only a Western student, inheriting Graeco-Roman concepts of "paganism" could be capable; the Muḥammadan view of Christianity as polytheism could be better justified than this.

In fact, if we consider Indian religious philosophy as a whole, and regard the extent to which its highest conceptions have passed as dogmas into the currency of daily life, we shall have to define Hindu civilization as one of the least superstitious the world has known. *Māyā* is not properly *de*lusion, but strictly speaking creative power, *śakti*, the principle of manifestation; *de*lusion, *moha*, is to conceive of appearances as things in themselves, and to be attached to them as such without regard to their procession.

In the *Bhagavad Gītā*, better known in India than the New Testament in Europe, we are taught of the Real, that "This neither dies nor is it born; he who regardeth This as a slayer, he who thinketh This is slain, are equally unknowing." Again and again, from the Upaniṣads to the most devotional theistic hymns the Godhead, ultimate reality, is spoken of as unlimited by any form, not to be described by any predicate, unknowable. Thus, in the Upaniṣads, "He is, by that alone is He to be apprehended" (cf. "I am that I am"); in the words of the Śaiva hymnist Māṇikka Vāçagar, "He is passing the description of words, not comprehensible by the mind, not visible to the eye or other senses." Similarly in later Buddhism, in the Vajrayāna (Śūnyavāda) system, we find it categorically stated that the divinities, that is, the personal God or premier angel in all His forms, "are manifestations of the essential nature of non-being"; the doctrine of the only reality of the Void (Behmen's "Abyss") is pushed to the point of an explicit denial of the existence of any Buddha or any Buddhist doctrine.

Again, whereas we are apt to suppose that the religious significance of Christianity stands or falls with the actual historicity of Jesus, we find an Indian commentator (Nīlakaṇṭha) saying of the Kṛṣṇa Līlā, believed historical by most Hindus, that the narration is not the real point, that this is not an historical event, but is based upon eternal truths, on the actual relation of the soul to God, and that the events take place, not in the outer world, but in the heart of man. Here we are in a world inaccessible to higher criticism, neither of superstition on the one hand, nor of cynicism on the other. It has been more than once pointed out that the position of Christianity could well be strengthened by a similar emancipation from the historical point of view, as was to a large extent actually the case with the Schoolmen.

As for India, it is precisely in a world dominated by an idealistic concept of reality, and yet with the approval of the most profound thinkers, that there flourished what we are pleased to call idolatry. Māṇikka Vāçagar, quoted above, constantly speaks of the attributes of God, refers to the legendary accounts of His actions, and takes for granted the use and service of images. In Vajrayāna Buddhism, often though not quite correctly designated as nihilistic, the development of an elaborate pantheon, fully realized in material imagery, reaches its zenith. Śaṅkâracārya himself, one of the most brilliant intellects the world has known, interpreter of the Upaniṣads and creator of the Vedânta system of pure monism accepted by a majority of all Hindus and analogous to the idealism of Kant, was a devout worshipper of images, a visitor to shrines, a singer of devotional hymns.

True, in a famous prayer, he apologizes for visualizing in contemplation One who is not limited by any form, for praising in hymns One who is beyond the reach of words, and for visiting Him in sacred shrines, who is omnipresent. Actually, too, there exist some groups in Hinduism (the Sikhs, for example) who do not make use of images. But if even he who knew could not resist the impulse to love, — and love requires an object of adoration, and an object must be conceived in word or form, — how much greater must be the necessity of that majority for whom it is so much easier to worship than to know. Thus the philosopher perceives the inevitability of the use of imagery, verbal and visual, and sanctions the service of images. God Himself makes like concession to our mortal nature, "taking the forms imagined by His worshipers," making Himself as we are that we may be as He is.

The Hindu Īśvara (Supreme God) is not a jealous God, because all gods are aspects of Him, imagined by His worshippers; in the words of Kṛṣṇa: "When any devotee seeks to worship any aspect with faith, it is none other than Myself that bestows that steadfast faith, and when by worshipping any aspect he wins what he desires, it is none other than Myself that grants his prayers. Howsoever men approach Me, so do I welcome them, for the path men take from every side is Mine." Those whose ideal is less high attain, indeed, of necessity to lesser heights; but no man can safely aspire to higher ideals than are pertinent to his spiritual age. In any case, his spiritual growth cannot be aided by a desecration of his ideals; he can be aided only by the fullest recognition of these ideals as retaining their validity in any scheme, however profound. This was the Hindu method; Indian religion adapts herself with infinite grace to every human need. The collective genius that made of Hinduism a continuity ranging from the contemplation of the Absolute to the physical service of an image made of clay did not shrink from an ultimate acceptance of every aspect of God conceived by man, and of every ritual devised by his devotion.

We have already suggested that the multiplicity of the forms of images, coinciding with the development of monotheistic Hinduism, arises from various causes, all ultimately referable to the diversity of need of individuals and groups. In particular, this multiplicity is due historically to the inclusion of all pre-existing forms, all local forms, in a greater theological synthesis, where they are interpreted as modes or emanations (*vyūha*) of the supreme Iśvara; and subsequently, to the further growth of theological speculation. In the words of Yāska, "We see actually that because of the greatness of God, the one principle of life is praised in various ways. Other angels are the individual members of a unique Self" (*Nirukta*, VII, 4): cf. Ruysbroeck, *Adornment* . . . , Ch. XXV, "because of His incomprehensible nobility and sublimity, which we cannot rightly name nor wholly express, we give Him all these names."

Iconolatry, however, was not left to be regarded as an ignorant or useless practice fit only for spiritual children; even the greatest, as we have seen, visited temples, and worshipped images, and certainly these greatest thinkers did not do so blindly or unconsciously. A human necessity was recognized, the nature of the necessity was understood, its psychology systematically analyzed, the various phases of image worship, mental and material, were defined, and the variety of forms explained by the doctrines of emanation and of gracious condescension.

In the first place, then, the forms of images are not arbitrary. Their ultimate elements may be of popular origin rather than priestly invention, but the method is adopted and further developed within the sphere of intellectual orthodoxy. Each conception is of human origin, notwithstanding that the natural tendency of man to realism leads to a belief in actually existent heavens where the Angel appears as he is represented. In the words of Śukrâcārya, "the characteristics of images are determined by the relation that subsists between the adorer and the adored"; in those cited by Gopālabhatta from an unknown source, the present spiritual activity of the worshiper, and the actual existence of a traditional iconography, are reconciled as follows—

"Though it is the devotion (*bhakti*) of the devotee that causes the manifestation of the image of the Blessed One (Bhagavata), in this matter (of iconography) the procedure of the ancient sages should be followed." [114]

The whole problem of symbolism (*pratīka*, "symbol") is discussed by Śaṅkarâcārya, Commentary on the Vedânta Sūtras, I, 1, 20. Endorsing the statement that "all who sing here to the harp, sing Him," he points out that this "Him" refers to the highest Lord only, who is the ultimate theme even of worldly songs. And as to anthropomorphic expressions in scripture, "we reply that the highest Lord may, when he pleases, assume a bodily shape formed of Māyā, in order to gratify his devout worshipers"; but all this is merely analogical, as when we say that the Brahman abides here or there, which in reality abides only in its own glory (cf. *ibid.*, I, 2, 29). The representation of the invisible by the visible is also discussed by Deussen, *Philosophy of the Upànishads*, pp. 99–101. Cf. also the discussion of *parokṣa* in Ch. V.

Parenthetically, we may remark that stylistic sequences (change of aesthetic form without change of basic shape) are a revealing record of changes in the nature of religious experience; in Europe, for example, the difference between a thirteenth-century and a modern Madonna betrays the passage from passionate conviction to facile sentimentality. Of this, however, the worshiper is altogether unaware; from the standpoint of edification, the value of an image does not depend on its aesthetic qualities. A recognition of the significance of stylistic changes, in successive periods, important as it may be for us as students of art, is actually apparent only in disinterested retrospect; the theologian, proposing means of edification, has been concerned only with the forms of images. Stylistic changes correspond to linguistic changes: we all speak the language of our own time without question or analysis.

Let us consider now the processes actually involved in the making of images. Long anterior to the oldest surviving images of the supreme deities we meet with descriptions of the gods as having limbs, garments, weapons or other attributes; such descriptions are to be found even in the Vedic lauds and myths. Now in theistic Hinduism, where the method of Yoga is employed, that is, focused attention leading to the realization of identity of consciousness with the object considered, whether or not this object be God, these descriptions, now called *dhyāna mantrams* or trance formulae, or alternatively, *sādhanās*, means, provide the germ from which the form of the deity is to be visualized. For example, "I worship our gentle lady Bhuvaneśvarī, like the risen sun, lovely, victorious, destroying defects in prayer, with a shining crown on her head, three-eyed and with swinging earrings adorned with diverse gems, as a lotus-lady, abounding in treasure, making the gestures of charity and giving assurance. Such is the *dhyānam* of Bhuvaneśvarī" (a form of Devī). To the form thus conceived imagined flowers and other offerings are to be made. Such interior worship of a mantra-body or correspondingly imagined form is called subtle (*sūkṣma*), in contradistinction to the exterior worship of a material image, which is termed gross (*sthūla*), though merely in a descriptive, not a deprecatory, sense.

Further contrasted with both these modes of worship is that called *para-rūpa*, "trans-form," in which the worship is paid directly to the deity as he is in himself. This last mode no doubt corresponds to the ambition of the iconoclast, but such gnosis is in fact only possible, and therefore only permissible, to the perfected Yogin and veritable *jīvan-mukta*, who is so far as he himself is concerned set free from all name and aspect, whatever may be the outward appearance he presents. Had the iconoclast in fact attained to such perfection as this, he could not have been an iconoclast.

In any case it must be realized, in connection with the gross or subtle modes of worship, that the end is only to be attained by an identification of the worshiper's consciousness with the form under which the deity is conceived: *nādevo devaṁ yajet*, "only as the angel can one worship the angel," and so *devo bhūtvā devaṁ yajet*, "to worship the Angel become the Angel." Only when the *dhyānam* is thus realized in full *samādhi* (the consummation of Yoga, which commences with focused attention) is the worship achieved. Thus, for example, with regard to the form of Naṭarāja, representing Śiva's cosmic dance, in the words of Tirumūlar,

The dancing foot, the sound of the tinkling bells,
The songs that are sung, and the various steps,

The forms assumed by our Master as He dances,
Discover these in your own heart, so shall your bonds be broken.

When, on the other hand, a material image is to be produced for purposes of worship in a temple or elsewhere, this as a technical procedure must be undertaken by a professional craftsman, who may be variously designated *śilpin*, "craftsman," *yogin*, "yogi," *sādhaka*, "adept," or simply *rūpakāra* or *pratimākāra*, "imager." Such a craftsman goes through the whole process of self-purification and worship, mental visualization and identification of consciousness with the form evoked, and then only translates the form into stone or metal. Thus the trance formulae become the prescriptions by which the craftsman works, and as such they are commonly included in the *Śilpa Śāstras*, the technical literature of craftsmanship. These books in turn provide invaluable data for the modern student of iconography.

Technical production is thus bound up with the psychological method known as *yoga*. In other words the artist does not resort to models but uses a mental construction, and this condition sufficiently explains the cerebral character of the art, which everyone will have remarked for himself. In the words of the encyclopaedist Śukrâcārya, "One should set up in temples the images of angels who are the objects of his devotion, by mental vision of their attributes; it is for the full achievement of this yoga-vision that the proper lineaments of images are prescribed; therefore the mortal imager should resort to trance-vision, for thus and no otherwise, and surely not by direct perception, is the end to be attained" (translated also above, p.114, in slightly different words).

The proper characteristics of images are further elucidated in the *Śilpa Śāstras* by a series of canons known as *tālamāna* or *pramāṇa*, in which are prescribed the ideal proportions proper to the various deities, whether conceived as Kings of the World, or otherwise. These proportions are expressed in terms of a basic unit, just as we speak of a figure having so many "heads"; but the corresponding Indian measure is that of the "face," from the hair on the forehead to the chin, and the different canons are therefore designated Ten-face, Nine-face, and so on down to the Five-face canon suitable for minor deities of dwarfish character. These ideal proportions correspond to the character of the aspect of the angel to be represented, and complete the exposition of this character otherwise set forth by means of facial expression, attributes, costume, or gesture. And as Śukrâcārya says further (see also more literal versions above, Ch. IV), "Only an image made in accordance with the canon can be called beautiful; some may think that beautiful which corresponds to their own fancy, but that not in accordance with the canon is unlovely to the discerning eye." And again, "Even the misshapen image of an angel is to be preferred to that of a man, however attractive the latter may be"; because the representations of the angels are means to spiritual ends, not so those which are only likenesses of human individuals. "When the consciousness is brought to rest in the form (*nāma*, "name," "idea"), and sees only the form, then, inasmuch as it rests in the form, aspectual perception is dispensed with and only the reference remains; one reaches then the world-without-aspectual-perception, and with further practice attains to liberation from all hindrances, becoming adept." [115] Here, in another language than our own, are contrasted ideal and realistic art: the one a means to the attainment of fuller consciousness, the other merely a means to pleasure. So too might the anatomical limitations of Giotto be defended as against the human charm of Raphael.

It should be further understood that images differ greatly in the degree of their anthropomorphism. Some are merely symbols, as when the Bodhi tree is used to represent the Buddha at the time of the Enlightenment, or when only the feet of the Lord are represented as objects of worship. A very important iconographic type is that of the *yantra*, used especially in the Śākta systems; here we have to do with a purely geometrical form, often for instance composed of interlocking triangles, representing the male and female, static and kinetic aspects of the Two-in-One. Further, images in the round may be *avyakta*, non-manifest, like a *liṅgam*; or *vyaktâvyakta*, partially manifest, as in the case of a *mukha-lingam*; or *vyakta*, fully manifest in "anthromorphic" or partly theriomorphic types.[116] In the last analysis all these are equally ideal, symbolic forms.

In the actual use of a material image, it should always be remembered that it must be prepared for worship by a ceremony of invocation (*āvahana*); and if intended only for temporary use, subsequently desecrated by a formula of dismissal (*visarjana*). When not in *pūjā*, that is before consecration or after desecration, the image has no more sacrosanct character than any other material object. It should not be supposed that the deity, by invocation and dismissal, is made to come or go, for omnipresence does not move; these ceremonies are really projections of the worshipper's own mental attitude toward the image. By invocation he announces to himself his intention of using the image as a means of communion with the Angel; by dismissal he announces that his service has been completed, and that he no longer regards the image as a link between himself and the deity.

It is only by a change of viewpoint, psychologically equivalent to such a formal desecration, that the worshipper, who naturally regards the icon as a devotional utility, comes to regard it as a mere work of art to be sensationally regarded as such. Conversely, the modern aesthetician and Kunsthistoriker, who is interested only in aesthetic surfaces and sensations, fails to conceive of the work as the necessary product of a given determination, that is, as having purpose and utility. Of these two, the worshipper, for whom the object was made, is nearer to the root of the matter than the aesthetician who endeavors to isolate beauty from function.[117]

Notes

Notes

1 (*page 5*). "A mental concept (*citta-saññā*) arises in the mind of the painter, that such and such a shape (*rūpa*) must be made in such and such a way. . . . All the various arts (*sippa*) in the world are produced by the mind," *Atthasālinī*, PTS. ed., p. 64; see "An Early Passage on Indian Painting," *Eastern Art*, III (1931), and cf. note 43.

2 (*page 6*). "Attracting form" is discussed in *JAOS.*, LII, 16, n. 8. Skr. *kṛṣ* (the root in *ā-karṣati*) has the same dual significance which is found in English "draw," as (1) to drag, drag toward or together, attract, and (2) delineate, draw up, compose, put in due form. English draw corresponds to G. *tragen*, to bear, and Skr. *dhṛ* (*dhar*) to bear, bear in mind, support, conceive, hold fast or firm, etc. While *kṛṣ* is to "draw" in either sense, *ā-kṛṣ* can be accurately rendered to "draw up" or "pro-duce." Cf. "fetch" (of the imagination), and "fetch" as an apparition. A remarkable use of English "draw" in our sense is to be found in Böhme's *Mysterium Pansophicum*, IV, 2 (which I can only cite in Earle's version), in connection with the formative aspect of the creative will (of God), as follows: "the desire is a stern attraction. . . . And it draws magically, viz. its own desiring into a substance" (cf. Skr. *dhar-ma*, as "substance").

3 (*page 6*). Upaniṣads, *passim*. Rabindranath Tagore retains the same phraseology in his song *Ami chini go chini*, where it is "in the immanent space of the heart" that he hears "now and again" the song of Bideśinī, the stranger lady who is ideal beauty — *hṛdi mājhe ākāśe sunecchi tomārī gān*. Where and what is this space in the heart? In the *Chāndogya Upaniṣad*, VIII, 14 (also VIII, 1, 1) *ākāśa* is called "the revealer of name and aspect," and identified with Brahman, the Imperishable, the Self. This

is "that mysterious nothing out of which the soul is made ... which nothing is *at large* in the almighty power of the Father" (Eckhart). This ideal space is the principle wherein all the possibilities of being can be realized (*Chāndogya Upaniṣad*, VIII, 1, 1–3). The *antarhṛdaya-ākāśa*, "space in the heart," is the totality of this ideal space at the innermost core of our being, where only the full content of life can be experienced in the immediately experienced; that consent, from the point of view of aesthetics, is "Beauty," from the point of view of epistemology "Truth" (cf. "Nirvāṇa is the transcendental knowledge of the sameness of all principles," *Saddharma Puṇḍarīka*, Kern's text, p. 133), and from the standpoint of ethics "Perfection." Thus while Beauty may be equated with Perfection and Truth absolutely (*rasa ... brahmâsvāda-sahôdara, Sāhitya Darpaṇa*, III, 1–2), loveliness is merely a good, ugliness merely an evil. Beauty is invisible and indivisible, only to be known as Deity is known, in the heart; art is an utterance of Beauty, science an utterance of Truth, ethics an utterance of Perfection in terms of light *and* shade, thesis *and* antithesis, good *and* evil. Error consists primarily in the attachment of absolute values to either of these relative factors, which are only means of apprehension, and not ends in themselves.

4 (*page 6*). *Bṛhadāraṇyaka Upaniṣad*, IV, 2, 3, with respect to the consent of essence and nature.

5 (*page 6*). "Contained in the Lotus of the Heart are Heaven and Earth ... both what is ours here and now, and what is not yet ours," *Chāndogya Upaniṣad*, VIII, 1, 1–3; "the Heart is the same as Prajāpati, it is Brahman, it is all," *Bṛhadāraṇyaka Upaniṣad*, V, 3; cf. *Ṛg Veda*, IV, 58, 11 and VI, 9, 6.

6 (*page 6*). The foregoing summary is based on a Sanskrit text cited by A. Foucher, *L'Iconographie bouddhique de l'Inde*, II (1905), 8–11; B. Bhattacharya, *The Indian Buddhist Iconography* (1924), 169 ff., and *Buddhist Esoterism*, 1932, Ch. XI;

and the *Bṛhadāraṇyaka Upaniṣad*, I, 4, 10. Cf. also the *Śukranītisāra*, IV, 4, 70–71, *above*, p. 113.

It will be observed that imagination (the power of having mental images) is here deliberately exercised. The vaguer implications of inspiration, enthusiasm, intoxication, are lacking. Needless to say, imagination may take form either as vision or as audition; what has been said above with reference to visual art applies equally to the case of literature, whether scripture or *belles lettres*. The Vedas, and all their accessory literatures and sciences, for example, are contained in the Word (*vāc*, *dharma*, *oṁ*), which having been uttered (*niḥśvasita*, *vyāhṛti*) is then heard (*śruti*) by the Prophets (*ṛṣi*), that audition depending not on "inspiration," but upon attention. Vālmīki, before he begins dictation, first visualizes in Yoga the entire *Rāmâyaṇa*, the characters "presenting themselves to his vision living and moving as though in real life"; and the work being thus completed before the practical activity is begun, the dictation is then so rapid that none but the four-handed Gaṇeśa, using all his hands, can take it down. Similarly, when the Bodhisattva attains Enlightenment, becoming Buddha, the Dharma presents itself to him in its entirety, ready to be taught, not merely as an idea to be subsequently developed. Similar conceptions of the operation of imagination are to be found already in the *Ṛg Veda*, where for example wisdom (*vāc*) is spoken of as "seen" or "heard" (X, 71, 4), ideas are "hewn out" √*takṣ*) "in the heart" (*hṛd*) (X, 71, 8), and thought is formulated (√*dhī*, cf. √*dhyai*, e.g. in *dhyāna*) as a carpenter shapes wood (III, 38, 1; cf. X, 51, 9–10, and Sāyaṇa on these passages).

The Indian formulation is idiomatic, but the process described is universal. The Scholastic parallels are very close; cf. Eckhart, "What I say springs up in me, then I pause in the idea, and thirdly I speak it out," again when he speaks of the carpenter who "first erects the house in his mind," or explains in what manner the Angels may be visualized (see *above*, p. 78). Cf. also Dante, when he says "I am one that when Love inspires me, pay heed; and in what way He dictates within me, that I speak out to you" (*Purgatorio,* XXIII, 53–54) and requires of his hearer to "hold the image like a firm rock" (*Paradiso,* XIII, 2–3, and it needs not to say that the author in the first place must have "held the image" thus); above all when he says "He who would paint a figure, if he cannot be it, cannot draw it" (*Convivio,* Canzone III, 53–54), glossed "No painter can portray any figure, if he have not first of all made himself such as the figure ought to be" (*Convivio,* IV, 10, 106, p. 309 of the Oxford text); again when he speaks of "figures as I have them in conception" (*Paradiso,* XVIII, 85); until finally the "high fantasy falls short of power" to depict the Deity as he is in himself (*Paradiso,* XXXIII, 142), as also in India *dhyāna* falls short of *samādhi,* failing to visualize the Brahman in any likeness, who is without likeness (*amūrta, nirābhāsa*) — *te contemplans totum deficit.*

Chuang Tzŭ (Giles, p. 240) gives an excellent account of the working of Yoga (though not so-called) in connection with the carpenter making a wooden stand for musical instruments, who, when asked, "What mystery is there in your art?" replies, "No mystery, your Highness, and yet there is something. When I am about to make such a stand . . . I first reduce my mind to absolute quiescence. . . . I become oblivious of any reward to be gained . . . of any fame to be acquired . . . unconscious of my physical frame. Then, with no thought of the Court present to my mind, my skill becomes concentrated, and all disturbing elements from without are gone. I enter some mountain forest. I search for a suitable tree. It contains the form required, which is afterwards elaborated. I see the stand in my mind's eye, and then set to work."

And as to habit (habitus, *tao* as "way"): "Let me take an illustration," said the wheelwright, "from my own trade. In making a wheel, if you work too slowly, you can't make it firm; if you work too fast, the spokes won't fit in. You must go neither too slowly nor too fast. There must be coördination of mind and hand. Words cannot explain what it is, but there is some mysterious art herein. I cannot teach it to my son; nor can he learn it from me. Consequently, though seventy years of age, I am still making wheels in my old age" (*ibid.*, p. 271). Similarly with the sword maker: "Is it your skill, Sir, or have you a way?" "It is concentration. . . . If a thing was not a sword, I did not notice it. I availed myself of whatever energy I did not use in other directions in order to secure greater efficiency in the direction required" (*ibid.*, p. 290).

7 (*page* 7). Dante's theory of art is discussed by Julius Schlosser, *Die Kunstliteratur* (Vienna, 1924), pp. 66–77. Dante's conception derives from Aristotle, St Thomas, and the troubadours, and is still essentially scholastic. In the *De Monarchia* he speaks of art as threefold, (1) as idea in the mind, (2) as technique in the tool (means), and (3) as potentiality in the material. In *Paradiso*, I, 127, he speaks of the *sorda* (*tāmasika*) quality in the material, which seems to resist the intention of the artist, recalling Eckhart's carpenter, who building a house "will first erect it in his mind and, were the house enough subject to his will, then, materials apart, the only difference between them would be that of begetter and suddenly begotten." Needless to say, Dante's *artista* includes those whom we now call artisans; see, for example, *Paradiso*, XVI, 49.

Dante in asserting the necessary identification of the artist with his theme (*chi pinge figura* . . ., as cited above) is still at one with the East and with Eckhart, as when the latter says, "On giving my whole mind to the subject of the angels . . . it seemed to me that I was all the angels," and "the painter who has painted a good portrait therein shows his art; it is not himself that it reveals to us." But Leonardo is already far removed from this point of view when he declares more than once, *il pittore pinge se stesso*, "the painter paints himself," "himself" not being the painter's essence, but the accidents of his being, his physiognomy, which come out in the painting just as a man is somewhat revealed in his handwriting. This inevitable reflection of the physical man in his handiwork is indeed also recognized in India, for example, *Lekhakasya ca yad rūpaṁ citre bhavati tād(rūp)yam*, "the painter's own shape comes out in the picture" (cited from a *Purāṇa*, *Rūpam* 27/28, p. 99); but this is precisely why the painter himself must be a normal man, since otherwise his peculiarity might be reflected in his art. From the Scholastic and Indian point of view, any such reflection of the person of the artist in his work must be regarded as a defect; whereas in later European art, the trace of the artist's individual peculiarities coming to be regarded as a virtue in the art, and flattering the artist's pride, the way to aesthetic exhibitionism and the substitution of the player ("star") for the play were prepared. In the same way the history of artists has replaced the history of art.

8 (*page 9*). See my *History of Indian and Indonesian Art*, p. 125; also, *Mahāvaṁsa*, XVIII, 24, XXVII, 10–20, and XXX, 11, and *Jātaka*, No. 489. For example, "vehicles" or "thrones," Skr. *vāhana, āsana*, which are living principles alike from the Christian and Hindu points of view (St Thomas, *Sum. Theol.*, I, Q. 108, A. 5–7; Garuḍa, Haṁsa and Nandi as the seats or vehicles of Viṣṇu, Brahmā, and Śiva); weapons or powers, Angels from the Christian, Devatās from the Hindu point of view (St Thomas, *ibid.*, *Bṛhad Devatā*, I, 74 and LV, 143); or the palaces and chariots (*vimāna, ratha*) of the Angels, imitated in their earthly shrines.

In *Mhb.*, XII, 285, 148, Śiva is called *sarva-śilpa-pravartaka*, "instigator of all arts," and *ibid.*, XIII, 18, 2 f., he imparts *kalā-jñāna*, "the understanding of accomplishments," to Garga. Observe that "Sanskrit" (*saṁskṛta*) is *deva-nāgarī*, "the language of the heavenly city," analogous to *deva-śilpāni*, the "angelic works of art" for which see *above*, pp. 8, 126.

With *Aitareya Brāhmaṇa*, VI, 27, cited in the text, cf. *Aitareya Āraṇyaka*, III, 2, 6, where "Prajāpati, the Year, after emanating offspring, was disintegrated (*viyasraṅsata*); he reintegrated himself (*ātmānaṁ samadadhāyat*) by means of the metres (*chan-*

dobhir)," and *Jaiminīya Upaniṣad Brāhmaṇa*, III, 11, where initiation is called a metrical transformation (*dīkṣate . . . chandāṅsy eva abhisambhavati*). In these passages the spiritual significance of rhythm in art is plainly asserted. Conversely they are also of interest in connection with the problem of the origins of art, all rhythm corresponding in the last analysis to cosmic rhythms; cf. *Jaiminīya Upaniṣad Brāhmaṇa*, I, 35, 7, "the Year is endless: its two ends are Winter and Spring. After (*anu*) this it is that the two ends of a village are united; after this that the two ends of a necklet meet"; *ibid.* I, 2, the *Gāyatra-sāman* "should be sung according to the course (*vartman*) of the Spirit and the Waters," and Jeremias, *Der Kosmos von Sumer*, 1932, p. 4, "Eine grosse Leistung Herman Wirths beruht darin, dass er in der Lehre vom Wege Gottes nach dem äonischen Lauf nicht nur die Wurzel der Symbolik gesehen hat — das war nicht neu — sondern auch die Wurzel der Sprache und Schrift."

9 (*page 9*). The Indian words *kalā*, *śilpa* both have the same broad significance that the word "art" once enjoyed in Europe; cf. New Oxford Dictionary, s.v. Art. I, "Skill in doing anything as the result of knowledge and practice," and II, "Anything wherein skill may be attained or displayed." A distinction is, however, to be made between the *śilpas*, or vocational arts, and the *kalās*, or avocational arts (accomplishments). It is not conceived that a *śilpa* can be acquired without training under a master (*ācārya*), or be practiced otherwise than as an hereditary profession. There are various lists of *śilpas*, generally eighteen in number, and always including architecture and painting. In the *Triṣaṣṭiśalākāpuruṣacaritra*, I, 2, 950 ff. (Gaekwar's Oriental Series, LI, 152), there is a list of "Five Arts (*śilpa*)," viz. those of the potter, architect, painter, weaver, and barber, each with its human *raison d'être* (*hetu*). For the sixty-four *kalās* see A. Venkatasubbiah, *The Kalās* (Inaug. Diss., Bern, Madras, 1911) (add to Bibliography L. D. Barnett, *Antagaḍa Dasāo*, p. 30); and A. Venkatasubbiah, and E. Müller, "The Kalās," *JRAS*. (1914).

There is a classification of the vocational arts (*sippa*) as elevated or respectable (*ukkaṭṭha*) and lesser or vulgar (*hīna*) in the *Vinaya*, IV, 6 f. There is also a distinction generally made in the dramatic *śāstras* between a high or cultivated (*mārga*) and a popular or folk (*deśī*) style of dancing, the former embodying *rasa, bhāva, vyañjanā*, etc., the latter consisting only of rhythmic movement, and being regarded (whether rightly or wrongly) as devoid of aesthetic content.

Thus it is hardly possible, except with the connotation "more or less expressive or significant," to speak of a distinction of arts according to their psychological quality or more or less honorable application; the distinctions that are made are rather with reference to the social status of the artist than with reference to the art itself, no professional artist having a high social status as such. Thus music and calligraphy are the highest arts in China because every gentleman and official is supposed to be proficient in them, while the painter, at least until the Sung period, was always regarded *qua* artisan, not *qua* gentleman. The sculptor, though his work served the highest ends of worship, was thought of only as an expert mason; and if in India he sometimes claimed a higher respect, this was not as artist in the modern sense, but because in setting up images he also exercised priestly functions, cf. *Mīmāṁsā Nyāya Prakāśa*, paragraphs 98, 229 (in Edgerton's edition, New Haven, 1929, pp. 78, 130). Although the drama and dancing belong to the most highly developed and sophisticated arts of Asia, the status of the professional actor has been generally no higher in Asia than it was in Europe in the time of Shakespeare.

It is generally true that a concept of vocation has always and everywhere prevailed in Asia, and that the practice of any art is foreordained by birth. There are, nevertheless, exceptions to all these generalizations, even to the extent that any art may be practiced gratuitously by an amateur as an avocation; for example, at the present day in Java some of the most expert actors are members of royal families, and the daughters of princes are accomplished dancers, and this was at one time also permissible in India. Standards in such cases are as high for the amateur as for the professional, but only the latter receives his social designation from his work. Here again it appears clearly that no kind of art is thought of as high or low, noble or ignoble in itself, only *persons* being considered of high or low rank according to their natal status in an established social hierarchy.

10 (*page 10*). *Nāṭya Śāstra*, I, 113 and 112 (Gaekwar's Oriental Series).

11 (*page 10*). *Sāhitya Darpaṇa*, VI, 2, and *Daśarūpa*, I, 7, IV, 47.

12 (*page 10*). For Hsieh Ho see note 19.

13 (*page 10*). For Seami's writings see A. Waley, *The Nō Plays of Japan* (1921), Introduction. Seami says, *Yūgaku no michi wa issai monomane ari*, "The arts of music and dancing consist entirely in imitation." That this does not mean imitation or naturalism of such sort as might, in the case of painting, be based on photographs of galloping horses is well shown in the following story about a particular performance:

In the Nō play *Tahusa*, the action of a player in the part of a reaper from Shinano was criticized by a spectator from Shinano as not corresponding to the actual usage of reapers in that district, that is, as not true to Nature. In the next performance the action was "corrected"; but the performance was a failure, for "it startled the eyes."

14 (*page 12*). The "Six Limbs" are given in Yaśodhara's twelfth- or thirteenth-century commentary on the *Kāma Sūtra*, Benares ed. (1929), p. 30, as follows:

"*Rūpa-bhedaḥ, pramāṇāni, bhāva-lāvaṇya-yojanaṁ*
Sādṛśyaṁ, varṇikā-bhanga, iti citraṁ ṣaḍangakaṁ,"

"Differentiation of types, canons of proportion, embodiment of sentiment and charm, correspondence of formal and pictorial elements, preparation (lit. "breaking," "analysis") of pigments, these are the six limbs of painting." For a more subjective interpretation see A. N. Tagore, *Sadanga, ou les Six Canons de la Peinture hindoue* (Paris, 1922).

The "Eight Limbs" of the *Samarâṅgaṇasūtradhāra* (see *JAOS.*, LII, 16, n. 8) are apparently *vartikā* (the crayon), *bhūmibandhana*, (? preparation of the ground), *rekhā-karmāṇi* (outline work), *lakṣaṇa* (characteristic lineaments of the types), *karṣa-karma* (production, perhaps = *varṇa-karma*, coloring), *vartanā-karma* (shading, that is, indication of plastic modelling, relievo), *lekha-karaṇa* (? corrections), and *dvika-karma* (? final outlines).

15 (*page 14*). See De, *Sanskrit Poetics*, II, 46–47. Sound and meaning (*rutârtha*) as "letter and spirit" are discussed from another point of view, that of the inadequacy of words, in the *Laṅkâvatāra Sūtra* (Suzuki, *Studies in the Laṅkâvatāra Sūtra* (1930), pp. 108, 113, 434, and see note 43). Sound is the physical fact, words are merely an indication, a hint, a pointing out the way — "do not fall into the error of thinking that the full meaning is contained in the letter"; meaning is a manner of inner perception, only to be divined by an activity of the intellect (*prajñā, buddhi*) in distinction from all associated ideas (*vāsanā*). The relation of this view to the *dhvani* theory of suggestion discussed below will be evident. But although words or other images are necessarily incomplete means of statement and communication, the given symbol may be perfect in the sense that it could not have been better found, just as the reflection of the moon in still water may be called perfect, though the moon is not in it otherwise than as an image. Just as the reflection is not substantially a doublet of the moon, so the work of art cannot be a doublet (*savarṇa*) of its subject, though it may be according to the workman's skill a perfect embodiment of the mental image present to his consciousness. The image whether in the mind or in the work is only a means to knowledge, not in itself knowledge.

Art in the artist is the indivisible identity of form and concept, formal and pictorial elements in his mind; art in the work is the embodiment of this identity in a given material. What is meant in either case by the "concomitance" (*sāhitya, sādṛśya*) of sound and sense, pictorial and formal elements, may be inferred from *Raghuvaṁśa*, I, 1, where Pārvatī and Śiva are spoken of as two-in-one, "commingled like a sound and its meaning," *vāgarthāv iva saṁpṛktau*; cf. Bhāmaha, I, 16, *śabdârthau sahitau kāvyaṁ*, "literature is the unity of sound and sense." Sound and sense, pictorial and formal elements, are the body of art, but these intelligible elements are not the soul (*ātman*) or ultimate content of art, as will appear later according to the theories of *rasa* and *dhvani*; and that is why according to Zen doctrine (and St Augustine) all scripture, in its finite sense, is vain.

The similar term *sārūpya*, "co-aspectuality," is used in connection with the theory of empirical (*pratyakṣa*) perception, where it is asserted (see Dasgupta, *History of Indian Philosophy*, I, 151 f., and Stcherbatsky, *Buddhist Logic*, II, 12 f. — my views agreeing with Stcherbatsky's rather than with those of de la Vallée Poussin in *Mélanges chinois et bouddhiques*, p. 415) that knowledge of an object presented to the senses consists in a coordination (*sārūpya* = *sādṛśya*) between the form assumed by the perceiving consciousness and the aspect presented by the object. The definition of *sārūpya* cited by Stcherbatsky, *loc. cit.*, I, 213, 552, and 555, viz. *atyanta-vilakṣaṇānām sālakṣaṇyam*, "similarity of things extremely dissimilar," corresponds exactly to the Nyāya-Vaiśeṣika definition of *sādṛśya* cited in our text, implying likeness by analogy. In any case, the terms (*sādṛśya, sārūpya, sāhitya, tadākāratā, anukṛti, anurūpa*, etc.) refer, not to likeness between things (symbol and referent, picture and model, to wit), but to a correspondence between ideas and things. This correspondence tends toward identity at higher levels of reference, but attains this identity only in the Absolute, experienced "like a flash of lightning" as *sādhāraṇya* and *sāyujya* in the consummation (*samādhi*) of contemplation (*dhyāna*).

That *sādṛśya* does not mean "visual resemblance" is further seen in the fact that *sādṛśya* is precisely that kind of "likeness" or "analogy" which is involved in metaphor (*upacāra*); cf. *Sāhitya Darpaṇa*, II, 10, "Metaphor (*upacāra*) consists in the suppression of what implies a difference of sense between two terms which are quite distinct from one another, viz. by means of an overplus of correspondence (*sādṛśya*) which brings them together." Classical examples of metaphor are *gaur bāhīkaḥ*, "a *bāhīka* (peasant) is an ox," and *agnir mānavakaḥ*, "the pupil is a fire."

Corresponding to *sādṛśya*, *sārūpya*, *tadākāratā*, *tadātmya*, etc., are *sādhāraṇya* (see note 47) and *sāyujya*, the consummation of Yoga in Identity. It will be seen that these terms are at the same time exact equivalents of the Scholastic *adaequatio*, and knowledge being an *adaequatio rei et intellectus*; "The knower," in the words of Eckhart (I, 394) "being that which is known."

Hsüan Tsang translates *sādṛśya* by *ch'ou* (2508), implying the notion of reciprocity. But it cannot be said that any Chinese terms actually used in aesthetics represent an exact equivalent of *sādṛśya*; and if one wished to coin such a technical term, *ying* (13294) *ch'ou* might be suggested.

16 (*page 14*). *Sāhitya Darpaṇa*, III, 19 and 20*a*, and *Daśarūpa*, IV, 52; cf. Regnaud, *La Rhétorique sanskrite*, p. 296. The actor may enjoy aesthetic experience (*āsvāda*) as the spectator of his own performance, not *qua* performer; cf. Śaṅkarâcārya, *Śataślokī*, 7, "Or does the actor, playing a woman's part (*strīveṣadhārī*) pant for a husband, imagining himself a woman?"

17 (*page 15*). *Pramāṇa*, from root *mā*, present also in English "measure," "mete," "metre," etc. On *pramāṇa* as principle see Masson-Oursel, *Une Connexion*, etc., and *Esquisse*, etc., pp. 256, 288. Thought of not as principle, but as ascertained standard,

pramāṇa can also be used in the plural, as "canon of proportion"; see note 14. It is essential to understand that even as "authority" *pramāṇa* must not be thought of as a measure possibly contradictory to experience; on the contrary, "correct" knowledge requires a coincidence, *consonantia*, of "theory" and "fact"; cf. note 15 as to *sādṛsya* and *sāhitya*, and Woodroffe, *Garland of Letters*, p. 266. Only *pramāṇa* conceived as an attribute or name of "God" or "Buddha" as "witness" (*sâkṣin*) can be called absolute; cf. Vasubandhu, *Abhidharmakośa*, VIII, 40 (Poussin, 222–225).

For Siam, cf. "The form (outline) of an object is judged by the standard of *drong* (proper forms in proper proportions) in accordance with *bāab* or example — referring to teachings of *āchāriya paramparā*" (pupillary succession), P. C. Jinavaravamsa, "Notes on Siamese Arts and Crafts," *Ceylon National Review* (July, 1907). An interesting analogy is presented by Zend *afsman*, generally "metre," but used in *Yasna*, XIX, as criterion or norm, with reference to right thought, right word, and right deed (*humatem, hukhtem, huarestem*).

18 (*page 18*). For Ching Hao see Waley, *Introduction*, etc., p. 169, and Sirén, *A History of Early Chinese Painting* (Index, *s.v.*). I may say that the text of the present work was completed and sent to press long before the appearance of Professor Sirén's admirable work in 1933; Sirén's book is probably the best account of Chinese aesthetics so far made available in a European language.

The two classes of painting here mentioned, viz. *shên* and *miao*, are the first two in the traditional threefold classification, *San p'ing*; see p. 18. Ching Hao has also two other classes, the Amazing (*ch'i*, 991) and the Clever or Skilful (*ch'iao*, 1411); the latter of these corresponds to the Accomplished (*nêng*, 8184) in the *San p'ing*. Cf. "This picture is clever (*ch'iao*) in composition and technique, but deficient in idea-movement (*i ch'ü*, 5367, 3120)."

19 (*page 19*). With Chinese *shên*, divine or spontaneous, compare also the remarks in notes 21 and 64, and Chuang Tzŭ on the Divine Man, Giles, *Chuang Tzŭ*, p. 151. *Shên-daiva*, "angelic."

Pratibhā, "illumination," is the usual designation of the poetic faculty. As to the nature of this faculty there is some difference of view. Some regard it as natural (*naisargikī*) or spontaneous (*sahajā*), or even supersensual (*lokôttarā*), making it one with the principle of form (*prajñā*) or with genius (*śakti*), and thus equivalent to Chinese *i* (5536), except that the Indian "genius" is not thought of in the European and Chinese way as functioning in rebellion against or apart from tradition. To sum up the views which are here and there expressed with varying degrees of emphasis in one direction or the other, one may say that the true artist is both born and made, both theoretically and practically equipped, by genius (*śakti*), imagination or vision (*pratibhā*), scholarship (*vyutpatti*), concentration (*samādhi*), and practice (*abhyāsa*). This is practically the view of the *Kāvyamīmāṁsā*. For the whole problem see De, *Sanskrit Poetics*, pp. 53, 369.

20 (*page 19*). The most elaborate discussion is by Petrucci. *Enclycopédie*, etc., pp. 7 ff., where the versions of Giles, Hirth, and Taki are also cited. Petrucci introduces into his interpretation a number of metaphysical ideas which are significant in themselves, but hardly justified by the text. My versions are based on Far Eastern sources kindly communicated by my friend and colleague Kojiro Tomita. The problems are also fully discussed in Sirén, *A History of Early Chinese Painting* (1933).

A connection of Hsieh Ho's Six Canons with Yaśodhara's Six Limbs (see note 14) has often been suggested. The difference of eight centuries in date does not exclude the possibility of derivation, for the Six Limbs represents nothing but a late list of ideas which were already current in India in the time of Hsieh Ho, and even as it stands may be a direct citation from older sources. However, it seems to me unnecessary to postulate any direct connection, and better to note simply the extent to which the Chinese and Indian ideas actually *correspond.*

In the first canon, the word *ch'i*, spirit, means from the Taoist point of view *life* as it proceeds from Heaven and Earth, the two modalities of the Tao, and even when understood as by Mencius in the sense of "passion-nature" or "fiery nature" represents the principle of life, as desire, the will to life. The word *ch'i* is also to be used with literal accuracy as the proper Chinese rendering of the third member of the Christian Trinity. The Indian equivalent is *prâṇa*, spiration, life, identified either directly with Brahman, or manifested as the Wind by which the Waters are stirred, so that his reflection which is the world-picture appears in them. *Ch'i* is accordingly "form" in the sense that "the soul is the form of the body"; or in the sense of desire or will to life, *ch'i* is represented by Indian *kāma* (Eros). Again, the idea *yün*, of operation or reverberation, is strictly comparable to what is meant by the *dhvani* of Indian rhetoricians (see note 49), it being only as it were by an echoing in the heart of the hearer that the full meaning of a word (or any other symbol) can be realized. The canon asserts that the ultimate theme of all art is the universal energy of the spirit, and for this point of view also many Indian parallels can be found, for example in the words of Kabīr (Bolpur, ed., I, 68) by "He is the true master (*sadguru*, or from the present point of view, true artist) who makes you perceive the Supreme Self (*paramâtman*) wherever the mind attaches itself." More theologically expressed, "Whatever may be apprehended by the mind, whatever may be perceived by the senses, whatever may be discerned by the intellect, all is but a form of Thee" (*Viṣṇu Purāṇa*, I. 4). Śaṅkarâcārya likewise asserts that art is a theophany (*ābhāsa*) when he says that Brahman is the theme equally of sacred and secular songs (Commentary on the *Brahma Sūtra*, I, 1, 20). Less metaphysically, in the *Viṣṇudharmottara*, XLIII, 39, it is asserted that he is a true painter who can represent the sleeping as possessed of life or sentience (*cetanā*), the dead as devoid of it.

The second canon asserts that the vehicle of expression (as defined in the first canon) is the brush stroke or line, and it is self-evident that the brush stroke or line is in itself the most abstract and intelligible part of the work, since an outline, boundary, or limiting plane does not correspond to anything *seen* in Nature but represents an interpretation of what we see; in other words, line is not representative, but symbolic. The same is implied by Indian authorities when they remind us that it is the line (*rekhā*) that interests the master, while the public cares most about color (see p. 101 and note 73). The third and fourth canons, taken by themselves, point out that the pictorial or representative elements in a work of art are those of shape (mass or area), and color, and this too becomes self-evident if we reflect that what the eye sees in Nature is nothing but a patchwork of colors, as was recognized early in the development of Indian psychology (see note 54); colored areas, being thus the primary data of sense impression, become in the work of art the primary means of recognition; and because the attempt at recognition is the first, animal, reaction of the naïve spectator, it has been observed that color is what interests the public (see p. 101 and notes 66 and 73).

Further, if we take the first and second pairs of canons together (as we are bound to do, because we must assume the consistency of the series) and assume the general Chinese and Indian principle of the conformity of a thing to its inner nature (for example, *Mṛcchakaṭika*, IX, 16, *na hy ākṛtiḥ susadṛśam vijahāti vṛttam*, "Outer-form by no means contradicts a like inward-disposition"; *Kumārasambhava*, v. 36, *pāpavṛttaye na rūpam*, "beauty goes not with evil nature" — Mallinātha cites *yatrā kṛtis tatra guṇāḥ*, "as are the forms, so are the virtues," and *na surūpāḥ pāpasamācārā bhavanti*, "the fair do not act sinfully"; *Daśakumāracarita*, Mitragupta's adventure, *seyam ākṛtir na vyabhicarati śīlam*, "Such is her person; the character must correspond"), what we have is tantamount to an assertion that the natural unity of a painting inheres in the conformity of its significance and its presentation, and this consent is precisely what we have already recognized (p. 13 and note 15) as *consonantia*, *sādṛśya*, etc. We have seen also that the same necessity is frequently enunciated in Chinese dicta on painting, and have suggested (note 15) that if a term should have to be coined, *ying* (13294) *ch'ou* (2508) might be suitable.

The fifth canon perhaps asserts only the necessity of placing the parts of a painting in their natural logical relation, or may be taken in connection with what has been said about composition, *above*, p. 20.

The last canon is not immediately equivalent to any one of the Six Limbs, but does correspond to what is met with throughout the theory and practice of art in India, *ch'uan* being equivalent to *śāstramāna*, *nāyāt*, *vidhivat*, *sippânurūpena*, etc. For example, it is "because of traditional authority (*nāyāt*) regarding them, displayed in treatises (*śāstrarūpatā*) compiled by learned men of modern times, that the arts (*kalā*), etc., are even today current (*vartate*)," *Triṣaṣṭiśalākāpuruṣacaritra*, I, 2, 972, the reference being to the preservation of the Five Arts and their subdivisions, alluded to in note 9.

21 (*page 22*). The visible (*dṛśya*, *viṣaya*) universe may be regarded as a real theophany, shining forth, *ābhāsa*, of God (cf. Chatterji, *Kashmir Shaivism* (1914), pp. 53–61, and Eckhart's "image-bearing light"), real to the extent that we perceive its ultimate significance, *paramârtha*. More empirically expressed, God is the creator, *nirmāṇa-kāraka*, of the world-picture, *jagaccitra*, of which the beauty, *ramaṇīyatā*, is the same as that which in art is the source of disinterested pleasure, *id quod visum placet*, *dṛṣṭi-prītiṁ vidhatte*. Śaṅkarâcārya himself uses the same simile, as follows: "On the vast canvas of the Self, the picture of the manifold worlds is painted by the Self itself, and that Supreme Self itself seeing but itself, enjoys great delight (*pramudaṁ prayāti*)" (*Svâtmanirūpaṇa*, 95). The world-picture is not here considered from the point of view of the practical activity as made up of lovely and unlovely parts, but as seen in contemplation, as an

aesthetic experience. For God is without motive or ends to be attained (*Bhagavad Gītā*, III, 22); his art is without means and not really a making or becoming, but rather a self-illumined (*svaprakāśa*), reflected modality (*ābhāsa*), or play (*līlā*), in which the gratuitous character of art attains its ultimate perfection. God is not visible in essence, but only as it were in regard, in the sensual world, according to the manner of our vision, which vision when perfected returns all creatures to their source, seeing them as He does.

This conception of God as the supreme artist, as representing the perfection toward which human art tends, has played an important part in both European and Asiatic aesthetics and theology. In Europe the idea has been current from the neo-Platonists onward, and was expressed with particular clarity by St Thomas and by Eckhart. These ideas are expressed in Chinese thought not merely by the term *shên* applied to art conceived as an unwilled manifestation, but also in the Taoist myths of the disappearance of the artist, and the coming to life of works of art, referred to in the text. These are in fact the inevitable consequences of perfection, that the artist becoming as God is no longer seen, and at the same time shares in the everlasting Now of God's timeless productivity. In Chinese Taoist tradition the attainment of perfection through art, as it were by *śilpa-yoga*, has received a specific mythical expression; but the idea of the necessary disappearance (*nivṛtta*, "involution," *abhisambhava*, "re-becoming") of the perfected being, however perfection may have been realized, naturally finds its place in all metaphysical systems. For example, *dhūtvā śarīram akṛtaṁ kṛtâtmā brahma-lokam abhisambhavāmi*, "Having shaken off the body (substance), as a self made (-perfect) I am conformed to the unmade world of Brahma," *Chāndogya Upaniṣad*, VIII, 13, where total realization is implied, involving a transformation even with respect to the intelligible plane. The notion recurs, of course, in the *Vedânta Sūtras*; cf. René Guénon, *L'homme et son Devenir selon le Vedanta*, pp. 194, 195. The disappearance or merging of the poet-saint Māṇikka Vāçagar in the image of Śiva (*Tiruvātavūrar Purāṇa*, VII, 28–29) affords a case in point. Cf. in the Hebrew tradition, Moses, Enoch, and Elias, the last of these appearing also in the Muhammadan tradition as having drunk of the Water of Life.

The equivalent in Christianity is the Ascension; cf. Eckhart: "We may reasonably suppose that when the time came for John to go, God caused to befall him what was due to happen on the day of judgment. . . . We may take it that his body, which was destined to perish here on earth, was disintegrated in the air, so that there entered into God only the being of his body, which would have accompanied the soul at the last day." The rationale of the disappearance proceeds immediately from the distinction of the sensible from the intelligible spheres of manifestation, Kāmadhātu or Kāmaloka, and Rūpadhātu or Rūpaloka (see note 74). The *śilpa-sthāna-kauśala*, or operative facility of the practical intellect, functions only on the sensible plane, where "work" is to be done; intellectual creation (*nirmāṇa*), functioning on both planes, (1) on the sensible plane is embodied by human will in a *work* of art, which "lives" and has "movement" only metaphorically, and (2) on the intelligible plane is immediately manifested as formal life. In any case, that art may be thought of as a "way" is most of all apparent in the fact that aesthetic perception is essentially disinterested.

22 (*page 24*). Recognition is not dependent on verisimilitude, but is by convention; the realistic spectator reverses the "imitative" procedure of the artist who has given form to natural shape, by interpreting the manufactured image (*rūpa*) as though it were the thing itself present to the eye (*pratyakṣa*) (Bhartṛhari, *Vākyapadīya*, III, 7, 5).

23 (*page 30*). In the *Lankâvatāra Sūtra, loc. cit.*, the unreality of appearances is illustrated by various similes, among them that of painted surfaces (*citrakṛta-pradeśā*) which are seen as if in relief (*nimnônnatā*), although really flat (*animnônnatā*).

24 (*page 32*). *Svapnavāsavadattā*, VI, 13, and *Mṛcchakaṭika*, IV, 0, 3. So also in *Mṛcchakaṭika*, IX, 16, *susadṛśa* is "true resemblance." Cf. *vṛddhisadṛśa*, "old-looking," in *Śukranītisāra*, IV, 4, 201, and *sadṛśa*, "the like" (= "etc."), in Vasubandhu's *Abhidharmakośa*, IX (Poussin, p. 275). For "exact likeness" we have also *tadānurūvaṁ* (*-rūpam*) in Haribhadra's *Āvaśyaka Ṭīkā*, II, 8, 2 and 3, and *pratyakṣam* in the *Karpūramañjarī*, I, 30.

In the *Viṣṇudharmottara*, III, 41, 2, *sādṛśya* is a noun, and *kiñcilloka-sādṛśya* must be taken to mean "in which there is a similitude only partially connected with the material world"; in any case nothing like an injunction to realism could be thought of, for the *satya* painting in question has clearly to do with the angelic sphere, and *pramāṇa* as well as *sādṛśya* are required in it. My version in *JAOS.*, LII, 13, needs correction accordingly; cf. my "Painter's Art in Ancient India; Ajaṇṭā," in *Journ. Indian Society of Oriental Art*, I, 26, n. 2.

25 (*page 38*). "Imagist" might perhaps be suitably rendered by *adhyavāsana*, "introsusceptive," *Sāhitya Darpaṇa*, II, 8–9.

Indian parallels to Zen are naturally not lacking; for example, in Jātaka, no. 460, the evanescence of the morning dew suffices to enlightenment, and analogous to the story of Tan Hsia is that of the Tamil poetess and devotee, Auvvai, who when she was rebuked for sitting with her feet outstretched towards the image in a temple, an act of formal disrespect, admitted her fault, but added, "If you will point out to me in what direction God is not to be found, I will there stretch out my feet." There are likewise abundant parallels in European tradition, for example in the Gospels, and in Eckhart and Blake.

26 (*page 39*). Chinese *ch'an* (348), Japanese *zen* = Sanskrit *dhyāna*, Pali *jhāna*.

27 (*page 41*). Version by Waley, italics mine.

28 (*page 43*). A Japanese *hokku*; in poems of this kind the hearer is expected to complete the thought in his own mind; cf. the Chinese phrase "to give spiritual form (*shên*) to the very part left undelineated," and what has been said above as to the literal inadequacy but practical efficiency of words (note 15), and below on the spectator's own effort (note 43).

29 (*page 44*). *Ukiyoye* means "pictures of the fleeting world"; the Japanese print is its typical product, but there are also paintings of the same kind.

30 (*page 45*). An allusion to the Persian Ṣūfī story of Lailā and Majñūn. When it was objected to Majñūn that Lailā was not so beautiful as he pretended, he answered, "To see the beauty of Lailā requires the eyes of Majñūn."

31 (*page 45*). Tiruveṅkaṭa's admirable preface to the Telugu edition (1887) of the *Abhinaya Darpaṇa* (see Coomaraswamy and Duggirala, *The Mirror of Gesture*, Cambridge, Massachusetts, 1917) may well be quoted here. Tiruveṅkaṭa first alludes to the neglect of the art and science of the mimetic dance (nautch) in modern times, which neglect had been mainly the result of European and puritanical influences, though he does not say as much, and then proceeds to a reassertion of the normal Hindu point of view:

"It is known to everyone that in these days our people not merely neglect this lore as though it were of a common sort, but go so far as to declare it to be an art that is only suited for the entertainment of the vulgar, unworthy of cultivated men, and fit to be practiced only by play-actors. But it is like the Union-Science (*yoga-śāstra*) which is the means of attaining spiritual freedom (*mokṣa*); and the reason why it has come to be regarded in such a fashion is that it is by movements of the body (*aṅgikâbhinaya*) that the lineaments and interplay of the hero and heroine, etc., are clearly exhibited, so as to direct men in the way of righteousness, and to reveal an esoteric meaning, obtaining the appreciation of connoisseurs and those who are learned in the lore of gesture. But if we understand this science with finer insight, it will be evident that it has come into being to set forth the sport and pastime of Śrī Krishna, who is the progenitor of every world, and the patron deity of the flavor of love (*śṛṅgāra-rasa*); so that by clearly expressing the flavor, and enabling men to taste thereof, it gives them the wisdom of Brahmā, whereby they may understand how every business is unstable; from which understanding arises aversion to such business, and therefrom arise the highest virtues of peace and patience, and thence again may be won the Bliss of Brahmā.

"It has been declared by Brahmā and others that the mutual relations of hero and heroine, in their esoteric meaning, partake of the nature of the relation of master and disciple, mutual service and mutual understanding; and therefore the Bharata Śāstra, which is a means to the achievement of the Four Ends of Human Life, Virtue, Wealth, Pleasure, and Spiritual Freedom, — and is a most exalted science, practiced even by the gods, — should also be practiced by ourselves."

32 (*page 45*). *Sāhitya Darpaṇa*, III, 9. *Vāsanā*, as "affect-ion," "perfuming," is the latent memory of past experience, and consequent present sensibility. Alike from the aesthetic and generally human point of view, *vāsanā* may be considered a necessary evil. Regarded as an affective aptitude, a liability to direct sympathy for, or prejudice on behalf of, ourselves or others, it represents a hindrance equally to enlightenment in general and to aesthetic experience in particular; but as the necessary basis for such ideal and disinterested sympathy as we feel at the spectacle of joy and sorrow represented in art, it is prerequisite to aesthetic experience. Cf. note 47.

The ideal character of poetic sensibility, that is to say the disinterested nature of aesthetic contemplation, is constantly insisted upon in the Alaṁkāra literature. It is pointed out, for example, in the *Sāhitya Darpaṇa*, III, 5 and 6, that even in the case of works of art of which the themes are in themselves distressing, no pain is felt by the spectator, but only delight, to which those who take intelligent delight in art bear unanimous witness.

33 (*page 46*). For *rasa*, etc., theories applied to painting or sculpture, see *JAOS.*, LII, 15, n. 5, and Basava Raja, *Śiva Tattva Ratnākara* (ed. Madras, 1927), VI, 2, 19.

34 (*page 46*). *Kāvya*, specifically poetry (prose or verse), also embraces the general idea of "art"; essential meanings present in the root *kū* include "wisdom" and "skill." One may compare Blake's use of "Poetic Genius" as equivalent to "Imagination" in the broadest sense of the word, and to the analogy of Greek *ποίησις*, denoting to the making of anything, for example, "creatures" or a ship.

35 (*page 46*). For example in the *Mālatīmādhava*, I, 33, 9–10, where the purpose of a portrait (*ālekhya-prayojana*) is consolation in longing (*utkaṇṭhāvinodana*), or *Priyadarśikā*, I, 3, where the play has "desired fruit," *vāñchita-phala*.

36 (*page 46*). *Sāhitya Darpaṇa*, I, 3. Cf. "As to the fact that the soul of poetry is flavor, and the like, there exists no difference of opinion" — *Vyaktiviveka*; and "All poetry lives by *rasa*" — Abhinavagupta.

37 (*page 47*). Meaning or utility is the indispensable motive of all art, but from the Indian point of view that is not art which does not also subserve the ultimate end of aesthetic experience, which is not so, or is so only to the most limited degree, in cases of bare efficacy, bare descriptive statement, or even "illustrative poetry," *citrakāvya*. For example, a piece of corrugated iron may keep out the rain, and may be called art inasmuch as it is a product of knowledge and technical skill, but it is scarcely a roof, architecturally speaking; in science, mere illustration and classification are scarcely art, but an elegant mathematical equation,

or any well-designed tool such as a telescope, is art. Any use of words or application of intelligence is art of a sort, but bare statement and efficacy are the crudest kind of art, not "primitive," but elementary, inasmuch as they are not far removed from functional exclamation. It is here if anywhere that a distinction of degree can be drawn between "fine" and "servile" art. But it is beneath the dignity of man to maintain his existence on a level of bare utility and functional necessity, and, as has been well said by Ruskin, "industry without art is brutality."

38 (*page 47*). To call a work of art *rasavat*, or ideally beautiful, is not strictly legitimate, but simply a manner of speaking and by projection, imputation, or inference (*anumāna*) or figuratively (*upacāra*); for it is constantly insisted that *rasa* is not an objective quality present in the work of art or any of its parts. Cf. Mukherjee, *Essai*, etc., p. 66; De, *Sanskrit Poetics*, II, 205, and note 43, below.

39 (*page 48*). *Sāhitya Darpaṇa*, III, 20*b*, ff.

40 (*page 48*). *Mālavikâgnimitra*, I, 4, *bhinna-rucer janasya*, "people of divers tastes."

"What Aesthetic, which implies thought and concept of art, can have to do with pure taste without concept is difficult to say," Croce, "The Breviary of Aesthetic," in *Rice Institute Pamphlet*, II (1915), 305.

41 (*page 48*). *Daśarūpa*, IV, 90. The opposite view, that art (especially drama, music, painting, and sumptuary arts) is nothing but a luxury, a tickling of the senses, is maintained only from a monastic, puritanical, and really naïvely materialistic view, mainly in early Buddhist and Jaina works, to a more limited extent in the *Dharma Śāstras*, and in modern times as a result of European influence; cf. note 31. Amongst Buddhist and Jaina texts might be cited *Brahma-Jāla Sutta*, I, 1, 13; *Visuddhi Magga*, 38; and *Āyāraṁga Sutta*, II, lect. 13.

42 (*page 50*). Cf. Maritain, *Introduction to Philosophy*, p. 263, n. 1: "the word *aesthetics* is derived etymologically from (the Greek word for) sensibility (αἰσνθάνομαι = feel), whereas art, and beauty also, are matters of the intellect, quite as much as of feeling." Were this more generally realized, much sentimentality in current thinking about art might be avoided.

43 (*page 50*). *Daśarūpa*, IV, 47, 50. Cf. *Laṅkâvatāra Sūtra*, II, 117, 118. *Raṅge na vidhyate citraṁ na bhūmau na ca bhājane . . . tattvaṁ hy akṣaravarjitam*, "the (real) picture is not in the color, nor in the surface, nor in the surroundings (but in the mind) . . . the principle transcends the letter." In this passage *bhājana may* be the painter's saucer of color, as means or material cause of the work, but more abstractly considered as "receptacle" means the environment of the work of art, or even the physical world; cf. the cosmos as *bhājana*, "receptacle," Vasubandhu, *Abhidharmakośa*, III, 44 (Poussin, p. 182 f.).

Cf. Confucius, *Analects*, XVII, xi, "Are bells and drums all that is meant by music?"; and Walt Whitman,

> All music is what wakes in you when you are reminded of it
> by the instruments,
> It is not in the violins and the cornets . . . nor the score of
> the baritone singer,
> It is nearer and further than they.

44 (*page 50*). Dharmadatta, cited in *Sāhitya Darpaṇa*, III, 9*a*, commentary.

45 (*page 51*). *Sāhitya Darpaṇa*, III, 2 and 3, and commentary; *Dhvanyālocana*, Nirṇaya Sāgara ed., p. 11.

46 (*page 51*). *Daśarūpa*, IV, 51; *Sāhitya Darpaṇa*, III, 19–20.

47 (*page 52*). *Sādhāraṇya* is analogous to empathy, *Einfühlung*; *vāsanā* ("perfuming") is innate or acquired sensibility, an emotional tendency which, though it may be developed as sentimentality, is nevertheless essential to the possibility of *sādhāraṇya* as ideal sympathy. *Sādhāraṇya* is another aspect of that

"consent" which we have already recognized as *sādṛsya, sāhitya, sārūpya, tadākāratā.*

To continue what has been said in note 32: aesthetic sympathy is ideal, without any ethical element; that is to say, it is felt equally with respect to good and evil, pleasure or pain, as represented. An ethical sympathy may indeed be legitimately felt with regard to such a hero as Rāma represented as a model of conduct in a poem, play, or painting, but such sympathy belongs to the proximate value of art in relation to *dharma*, not to aesthetic appreciation (*āsvāda*), wherein the spectator sees as if with the eye of God, who "regards neither the good nor the evil works of anyone" (*Bhagavad Gītā*, V, 15), but "makes his sun to shine alike upon the just and the unjust," for "the vision of God transcends virtues," Eckhart, I, 273. The impartiality of aesthetic reproduction, the fact that art as such is related rather to law than to equity, is well brought out in the *Nāṭya Śāstra*, I, 112 ff.; see translation in the *Mirror of Gesture*, p. 2.

48 (*page 52*). *Daśarūpa*, IV, 45.

49 (*page 53*). *Dhvani* is literally "sound," especially sound like that of thunder or a drum, hence "resonance" or "overtone" of meaning. A striking analogy can be found in the first canon of Hsieh Ho as written with the character *yün* (13843), that the essential in art is "the reverberation (*yün*) of the spirit in the forms of life," the idea of sound*ing* rather than of mere sound being present both in *dhvani* and in *yün* (13843). Significant synonyms of *vyañjanā*, lit. "revealing," are *dhvanana*, "echoing," and *gamana*, "motion." As to the latter, it may be observed that when anything is spoken of as represented in an image, it is said to be *citragata*, "gone into representation"; cf. Eckhart, "to be properly expressed, a thing must proceed from within, moved by its form," and Leonardo, "That drawing is best which best expresses the passion that animates the figure." *Vyañjanā*, however, viz. in Buddhist usage, means only the "letter" as opposed to the "spirit" or "meaning" (*attha* = *artha*). The later

sense endows the "letter" with a suggestive significance beyond the literal.

50 (*page 53*). See Dhvanikāra, *Dhvanyālokalocana* ("The Eye of Perception of Content"), cited by Mukherjee, *Essai*, etc., pp. 85–90.

51 (*page 54*). From the point of view of the *Laṅkâvatāra Sūtra*, the two chief hindrances are *kleśâvaraṇa* (sensual attachment) and *jñeyâvaraṇa* (mental or systematic hindrances), one might say affections and prejudices. Cf. Blake, "man has closed himself up. . . . If the doors of perception were cleansed, all things would appear as they are, Infinite." It must be borne in mind that from the Indian point of view enlightenment and perfection are always virtually present, that is, not to be *acquired* by any means but only to be *revealed* when the mirror of the soul is cleansed from dust. This is a metaphor particularly applicable in the aesthetic field; aesthetic contemplation cannot be taught; all that can be done is to break down the barriers that stand in the way of realization.

52 (*page 56*). A clear distinction is here drawn between the functional means of perception as they are in themselves (for example, the eye's intrinsic faculty), and their use determined by intelligence; voice (*vāc* = *viṣaya śabda*) in this passage is to be distinguished from speech (*vāc*) in the *Bṛhadāraṇyaka Upaniṣad*, IV, 1, where speech is identified with discrimination or pure intellect (*prajñā*), and in *Chāndogya Upaniṣad*, VII, 2, where speech "makes known" name.

"Name and aspect" (*nāma-rūpa*) are the fundamental conventions (respectively intelligible and sensible) by which phenomena are knowable (discriminated). Thus in the *Śatapatha Brāhmaṇa*, XI, 2, 3, name and aspect are treated as the two manifestations of the Brahman, whereby He is known in the contingent universe, "aspect being intellect, inasmuch as it is by intellect that one seizes aspect," and "name being speech, inasmuch as it is by speech that one seizes name," and these two are not distinguishable in nature, for "whatever is name is indeed aspect." The last passage really asserts the identity in principle of all arts; cf. Eckhart, "form is a revelation of essence" (380) and "the soul knows only in effigy." Further, "As far as there are name and aspect, so far indeed extends this world" (*Ś. Br.*, *ibid.*). Cf. *Kauṣītaki Upaniṣad*, I, 3, where Mānasī and Cākṣuṣī, "Intelligence" and "Perception," are personified as the consorts of Brahma and immediate causes of the phenomenal universe. But in Brahman, called Spectator or Overseer (*paridraṣṭṛ*), name and aspect as human modes of perception and representation are transcended (*Praśna Upaniṣad*, VI, 5). There are in fact three modes of vision, that of the functional fleshly eye (*māṁsa-cakṣu*), the angelic eye (*divya-cakṣu*, the intellect), and the eye of transcendent wisdom (*prajñā-cakṣu*, gnosis), respectively functional, all-seeing, and seeing in simultaneity. The last is the third eye of Śiva, which destroys, or rather trans-forms, appearance by its non-perception of duality. So, in the last analysis, "It is not aspects that one should seek to understand, but the Seer (*draṣṭṛ*) of aspects" (*Kauṣītaki Upaniṣad*, III, 8): "seeing Whom, nought else remains to be seen, *yad dṛṣṭvā nāparaṁ dṛśyam*" (Śaṅkarâcārya, *Ātmabodha*, 55). He who thus attains the world of Brahman becomes a "Seer without duality (*draṣṭā advaitaḥ*), this is man's highest path, his highest bliss, etc." (*Bṛhadāraṇyaka Upaniṣad*, IV, 3, 32).

It should be noticed once for all that, just as in English, so in Sanskrit very many words, for example *vāc*, *rūpa*, are necessarily used in two senses, empirical and ideal, or even in three senses, literal, ideal, and transcendental. *Rūpa*, however, when correlated with *nāma*, has always to be rendered by "aspect" rather than by "form"; it is really *nāma*, "name," or "idea," that is the determining principle or "form" of the species. Thus with respect to man, *nāma-rūpa* is "soul and body"; the soul being the "form" of the body. To render *nāma-rūpa* by "name and form" is tautological.

For the distinction of speech from sound cf. Chuang Tzŭ: "Speech is not mere breath. It is differentiated by meaning" (Giles, *Chuang Tzŭ*, 1889, p. 16).

53 (*page 56*). *Ibid.*, IV, 1, 7, the heart (*hṛdaya*) is said to be the support of all things, the highest Brahman; cf. note 3. The heart is thus a synonym for the centre and entirety of being. This has to be borne in mind in connection also with the term *sahṛdaya*, "having heart," equivalent to *rasika* and *pramātṛ*.

54 (*page 56*). *Atthasālinī*, p. 317; Woodward, *Gradual Sayings*, I, 159, n. 2; Keith, *Buddhist Philosophy*, p. 169.

55 (*page 61*). Maritain, *Art and Scholasticism*, p. 1.

56 (*page 61*). Meister Eckhart was born in Saxony or Thuringia about 1260. He became a professor in Paris, and later held very high clerical positions in Bohemia and Germany. He was suspected of heresy, and condemned in 1329, two years after his death. He taught not in Latin but in the vernacular, and has been called the father of the German language. St Thomas had died (1274) while he was still a youth; Tauler and Ruysbroeck were his contemporaries, and had probably heard him preach. The materials cited in the present essay are derived from *Meister Eckhart*, translated by C. de B. Evans from Franz Pfeiffer's collected German edition of 1857, in two volumes, London, 1924 and 1931; the page references are to the first volume unless otherwise stated.

Eckhart presents an astonishingly close parallel to Indian modes of thought; some whole passages and many single sentences read like a direct translation from Sanskrit. See from this point of view R. Otto, *Mysticism East and West* (New York, 1931), and my *New Approach to the Vedas* (London, 1934).

It is not of course suggested that any Indian elements whatever are actually present in Eckhart's writing, though there are some Oriental factors in the European tradition, derived from neo-Platonic and Arabic sources. But what is proved by the analogies is not the influence of one system of thought upon another, but the coherence of the metaphysical tradition in the world and at all times.

57 (*page 62*). In this respect, Eckhart's nearest and natural descendant is Blake; for example, Jesus and his Disciples were all Artists; Praise is the Practice of Art; Israel delivered from Egypt is Art delivered from Nature and Imitation; The Eternal Body of Man is the Imagination; The gods of Greece and Egypt were Mathematical Diagrams; Eternity is in love with the productions of time; Man has no Body distinct from his Soul; If the doors of perception were cleansed, all things would appear to man as they are, infinite; In Eternity All is Vision.

58 (*page 62*). Cf. *tridhā, saṁhitā* in the Upaniṣads, for example *Bṛhadāraṇyaka Up.*, I, 2, 3 and *Taittirīya Up.*, I, 3, 1–3.

59 (*page 64*). All ritual, offices, and sacraments (*pūjā, yajña, saṁskāra*) are art. For transubstantiation see Eckhart, 87, 477: "the sacrament nourishes like any other food. But it has none of the nature of bread" (477), just as with other works of art, which may please any sense, but are to be taken in another sense, allegorical or anagogic. The Catholic view is that though a man may be drawn to any work of art (such as scripture) *causa voluptatis*, he may well proceed *rationem artis intelligere*. Cf. *Laṅkâvatāra Sūtra*, II, 118, 119, where a painting is said to be produced in colors "for the sake of attracting (*karṣaṇa*) spectators," though the very picture is not in the colors (*range na citram*), but subsists as the art in the artist, and by the spectator's own effort again as art in him.

60 (*page 72*). Leonardo's *il pittore pinge se stesso*, perhaps the first enunciation of the principle on which depends the validity of the modern game of attribution.

61 (*page 78*). This point of view still survives in Dante's *Chi pinge figura, si non può esser lei, non la può porre.*

62 (*page 84*). Deliberate conventionalizing, calculated search for the abstract or so-called ideal, as in the modern practice of designing, and in archaism, is a different activity, not a "singling out the best" I *can*, but what I *like* best.

63 (*page 88*). "The heathen philosopher Aristotle says, 'Were there no house nor place and no materials it would be all one being, one matter, which being divided is like another soul'" (II, 290).

St Thomas (*Sum. Theol.*, III, Q. 23, A. 3): "the form of a house already built is like the mental word of the builder in its specific form, but not in intelligibility, because the material form of a house is not intelligible, as it was in the mind of the builder."

64 (*page 91*). Human nature as it is in God "does not appear in the looking-glass image . . . only just the features are seen in the mirror" (51), the features being the accidents of being, not the man as he *is*. Cf. the Chinese phrase for portraiture, *fu shên*, "portraying the divine image in a man."

The history of portraiture in Europe provides an interesting and rather unhappy contrast to the Chinese and Indian notions of *fu shên*, "portraying soul," and *sva-rūpa*, "intrinsic aspect." In what follows, quotations are from Jitta-Zadoks, *Ancestral Portraiture in Rome* (Amsterdam, 1932), pp. 87, 92 f. The tendency to realism and the use of death masks are "two coördinate consequences of one and the same mentality. . . . This mentality will bring about as well portraits of extreme realism (so-called verism) as the practice of making moulds on the actual features" of the living model. Now, tomb effigies came into use about 1200: "These statues first represented the deceased not as he actually appeared after death but as he hoped and trusted to be on the day of Judgment. This . . . is apparent in the pure and happy expression of all the equally youthful and equally beautiful faces which have lost every trace of individuality. But towards the end of the XIIIth century . . . interest turned from the heavenly Future to the worldly Present. Not how the dead would perhaps appear one day but how they had actually been in life was considered important. More or less likeness was now wanted. . . . As the last consequence of this demand for exact likeness the death mask, taken from the actual features, made its appearance . . . rationalism and realism appearing at the same time. . . . The death mask . . . really did help the artist to draw near to Nature and this it achieved by teaching him the construction of the face . . . (at last) . . . the head is constructed from within and is created by the artist as by Nature herself." The history of post-Renaissance European art thus takes on the aspect of a reanimation of the corpses in a charnel house (cf. *Speculum*, April, 1933, Pl. XI), rather than that of a Resurrection of the Dead in a more glorious form. One begins to see why Śukrâcārya could speak of portraiture as *asvargya*. "Portraiture belongs to civilisations that fear death" (Kramrisch, *Indian Sculpture*, p. 134).

With respect to the representation of the deceased, not as they may have looked in real life but as they "hoped and trusted to be on the day of Judgment," compare (1) the Indian, and more typically Cambodian and Javanese, practice of representing deceased ancestors in the form of the deity to whom they had been devoted, and (2) in the *Saddharma Puṇḍarīka* the resurrection of past Buddhas and Bodhisattvas in glorified bodies — iconographic representations always reproducing the "exemplary elements" or lineaments (*lakṣaṇa*) of these glorified bodies, rather than any of those individual accidents by which the man might have been recognized at the time of his earthly ministry.

65 (*page 100*). For the full context see Coomaraswamy and Duggirala, *The Mirror of Gesture*, pp. 14, 15.

66 (*page 101*). It is possible, therefore, that in making *varṇâḍhya* Duryodhana's first exclamation some sarcasm is intended.

67 (*page 103*). Cf. *Triṣaṣṭiśalākāpuruṣacaritra*, I, 1, 360, where a man whose eyes are fastened to the (? painted) forms of beautiful women, etc., is said to stumble (*skhalati*), as if the border of his

garment had been caught on a hedge. Cf. "there is no actual relief in a painting, and yet we see it there," *citre . . . natônnataṁ nâsti ca, dṛśyate atha ca, Mahāyāna Sūtrâlaṁkāra*, XIII, 17; cf. *Laṅkâvatāra Sūtra* and see note 23.

In the *Śakuntalā*, the "hills and vales" may be either those of the bodies of beautiful women represented in the picture, *nimnônnata* having this application in *Mālatīmādhava*, IV, 10, or those of the landscape background, *pradeśa* having this sense in the *Śakuntalā* itself, *infra*, VI, 19, and perhaps also in *Laṅkâvatāra Sūtra*, p. 91.

68 (*page 104*). Viz. *rūpa-śobhā*, as in *Divyâvadāna*, p. 361.

69 (*page 106*). Similarly in the case of the dancing competition, *Vikramacaritra*, *HOS.*, XXVII, 15, the two apsarases first dance together and the assembly of the gods is delighted, *nṛtyaṁ dṛṣṭvā saṁtoṣam agamat.*

70 (*page 106*). The text here, vv. 4, 5, and 6, is almost identical with *Mālavikâgnimitra*, II, 3, 6, and 8.

71 (*page 107*). "Judgment" is *vivādanirṇaya.* In the *Mālavikâgnimitra*, the King as connoisseur is *viśeṣajña*, as judge, *praśnika.*

72 (*page 107*). Ryder, in *HOS.*, IX, 44, renders admirably the substance of Cārudatta's remarks, but with a European nuance and avoiding all the technicalities. The *Mṛcchakaṭika* passage is anticipated in a briefer form in Bhāsa's *Daridra-Cārudatta*, II, 2.

73 (*page 108*). It is constantly brought out that craftsman and critic attach principal importance to the drawing, by which the moods are expressed, but that what the public cares about is color. As Binyon has observed, "The painting of Asia is throughout its main tradition an art of line."

74 (*page 109*). The nearest to anything of this kind in connection with the formative arts occurs in *Jātaka*, VI, 332, where the Bodhisattva employs a master-architect (*mahā-vaḍḍhaki*) to build a hall such as he requires.

The master-architect does not grasp the Great Being's idea (*mahāsatta-cittaṁ na gaṇhati*), and when corrected explains that he can work only according to the tradition of the craft (*sipp-ânurūpena*), and knows no other way (*aññatha na jānāmîti*). The Bodhisattva himself then lays out the plan "as if Viśvakarma himself had done it." Even so, the form of the hall is determined entirely by the use to which it is to be put; the Bodhisattva's plan is not a personal whim or a piece of self-expression, it is simply that he knows better than the architect all that is present to the mind of the divine craftsman, the "All-maker."

This supernatural virtuosity (*kauśala*) of the Bodhisattva is described in the *Lalita Vistara*, Ch. XII: it is a command of the arts not acquired by study, *na ca . . . yogyā kṛtā . . . śilpakauśalam* (Lefmann's ed., p. 156, l. 1). Cf. the *Mahāyāna Sūtrâlaṁkāra* of Asaṅga, VII, 6, where the sage (*dhīragata*, "who has become a seer") is said to exhibit a threefold *nirmāṇa*, "manifestation" or "facility," the first of these being displayed in the field of art (*śilpakarma-sthāna*).

More fully in Vasubandhu's *Abhidharmakośa*, II, 71–72 (Poussin, p. 320), virtuosity (*kauśala*) in art (*śilpa-sthāna*) and the power of mental creation are two of the four mental activities exhibited by a perfected being on the sensible plane of manifestation (*Kāmadhātu, Kāmaloka*). Of these two, the *śilpa-sthāna-kauśala*, or facility of the practical or operable intellect, is naturally absent on the intelligible plane of manifestation (*Rūpadhātu, Rūpaloka*), while both, of course, are absent on the supersensual super-rational plane of non-manifestation (*Dharmadhātu, Arūpyaloka*). . . . The same idea is expressed in another way by the attribution of an absolute *pramāṇa* to the perfected being, all other *pramāṇas* being merely as to what is correct under certain circumstances; see note 17.

There are some minor references to originality in poetry. Thus, Rājaśekhara, *Kāvyamīmāṁsā*, XI (see De, *Sanskrit Poetics*, II, 373), discussing plagiarism (*haraṇa*, "theft") at some length, says that the great poet (*mahākavi*) depicts something new (*nūtana*) in meaning and expression as well as what is old; and flagrant stealing (*pariharaṇa*) is called unpoetical or inartistic, *akavitvadāyi*. An example occurs in the *Karpūramañjarī*, III, 31, where the King compliments the heroine on her verses, remarking on her seizure (*daṁsaṇa*) of new motifs (*nava-vastu*), varied vocabulary (*ukti-vicitratva*), and sense of beauty (*ramaṇīyatā*) and on the flow of *rasa*.

75 (*page 113*). The printed text is that cited by Paṇḍit Jībânanda Vidyāsāgara (Calcutta, 2nd ed., 1890). The only complete translation is that of Benoy Kumar Sarkar, *The Sukranīti* (Allahābād, 1914, *Sacred Books of the Hindus*, Vol. XII). An introduction to this translation, by Dr. (Sir) Brajendranath Seal, entitled *The Positive Background of Hindu Sociology*, forms vols. XVI and XXV in the same series.

76 (*page 117*). Masson-Oursel, "Une Connexion dans l'Esthétique et la Philosophie de l'Inde," *Rev. des Arts Asiatiques*, II, (1923), and H. Zimmer, *Kunstform und Yoga im indischen Kultbild* (Berlin, 1926).

77 (*page 117*). A. K. Coomaraswamy, "Nāgara Painting," *Rūpam* 37, 40 (1929), and *Viṣṇudharmottara*, III, 41, *JAOS*., LII (1932).

78 (*page 122*). In English, we often distinguish *parokṣa* terms by capitals; for example, in distinguishing Self from self, both represented in Skr. *ātman*, or when we distinguish Cross as symbol from such crosses as are represented in the letter x.

79 (*page 123*). *yasmād devāh*, Śaṅkarâcārya on *Ait. Up*., III, 14; more freely translated, "for, indeed, just what the Angels are is Pure Intelligences."

80 (*page 125*). Cf. *Bṛhadār. Up*., I, 4, 17, "Verily by perception (*cakṣuṣā*) He comes into possession of his human (*mānuṣa*) possessions (*vitta*)."

81 (*page 125*). Iconography (*pratimākaraṇa*) as art in being is to be distinguished from iconography (*rūpa-bheda*) as a science, useful or necessary to the artist or student.

82 (*page 126*). *Anukṛti* is "imitation" in the sense *Ars imitatur naturam in sua operatione*, which does *not* mean *imitatur entem naturatam*, our environment.

The same notion is implicit in many passages of the *Ṛg Veda*; for example, V, 2, 11, where the artistry of the incantation (*mantra*, cf. *mantrayanti* with reference to angelic intercommunication, *ibid.*, I, 164, 10) is compared to that of a carpenter or weaver.

83 (*page 126*). A point of view equating "criticism" and "reproduction" may be represented here, as it is certainly in later Indian aesthetic.

84 (*page 126*). *Psychological Types*, p. 601.

85 (*page 127*). "Nature" here in the popular sense of *ens naturata*, phenomenal environment. The "worship of Nature" in this sense implies "pantheism." Needless to say that "Nature," interpreted at a higher level of reference, viz. as *natura naturans* (= *prakṛti*, *māyā*, etc.), and "Nature" as the "Mother of the Son of God" have both the same reference (it is by Her that He takes on human nature). "To find nature herself" (in this sense) "all her likenesses must be shattered" (Eckhart). That iconoclasm may be accomplished in two different ways, respectively *parokṣāt* and *pratyakṣeṇa*: in the first case, intellectually, by making the proper references, in the second case, brutally, by a literal "destruction of idols."

86 (*page 129*). His intrinsic manifestation (*svarūpa*) is the manifestation of very different things (*viśvarūpa*).

87 (*page 130*). When the Lord (*īśvara*) is spoken of in His unitary aspect, the Spoken Word is single.

88 (*page 131*). Inasmuch as Wisdom is measured out into parts, it cannot be argued that "close hidden" means only *in potentia*, in the Godhead, Para-Brahman, *solus ante principium*, *pūrṇa apravartin*, where things are not even "thought" under the con-

tingent aspect of distinction. "Hidden," etc., is tantamount to *in principio*.

89 (*page 133*). *Ghana*, from *ghan*, to strike, hinder, etc., has a primary sense of "dense mass," implying a condensation of multiple factors without extension in space. Hence "mere" or "essential": or *prajñāna-ghana* might be more freely rendered as "exemplary understanding."

90 (*page 134*). Cf. my "Parāvṛtti = Transformation, regeneration, Anagogy," in *Festschrift Ernst Winternitz*, 1933.

91 (*page 136*). In what follows, the *pratyakṣa* notions are again distinguished by italics.

92 (*page 136*). G. Dandoy, S. J., *L'Ontologie du Vedânta* (Paris, 1932), p. 125.

In *Bṛhadār. Up.*, III, 4, 2, Hume renders *sâkṣāt aparokṣa* (equivalent to *paramârthika pratyakṣa*) by "present and not beyond our ken." But the meaning is "immediately," not as thus implied, "objectively." "Not beyond our ken" belies the sense; the Brahman, who is the Self in us and all things (as is emphasized in the text itself) cannot be an object of knowledge.

Suzuki, *Laṅkâvatāra Sūtra*, p. xxvi, renders (*paramârthika-*) *pratyakṣa* by "intuitive penetration."

Stcherbatsky, *Buddhist Logic*, II, 284, translating a passage from Vācaspatimitra in which the presumed identity of an object known in the past and in the present is under discussion, renders *parokṣa*, qualifying the previous cognition, as "transcends the ken," and *aparokṣa*, qualifying the present cognition as "does not transcend the ken," and this in the given context seems to be quite legitimate. Again, *ibid.*, p. 333, n. 1, "objects are divided into (1) evident facts (*pratyakṣa*), (2) inferred facts (*parokṣa*) of whom (*sic*) we have formerly had some experience, (3) very much concealed facts (*atyanta-parokṣa* = *šin-tu-lkog-pa*) which are either transcendental, unimaginable entities, or else facts never experienced, but nevertheless not unimaginable."

Mānasa-pratyakṣa is "attention" (Stcherbatsky, loc. cit., II, 328, n. 2).

Muir, Sanskrit Texts, IV, 22, renders *parokṣa* "esoterically." "Paradoxical," "enigmatic," or "mysterious" would be satisfactory renderings only if taken in their strictly technical senses.

93 (*page 137*). We do not think of the technical language of a special science as "obscure," or even as "cryptic" or "esoteric," merely because as laymen we may not understand it. Though metaphysics is not a special science, the analogy holds good.

94 (*page 137*). *Guhya* ("hidden") is often the equivalent of *parokṣa*: e.g. in *Ṛg Veda*, V, 5, 10, "Where-e'er it be, O Vanaspati (Agni), that thou knowest the hidden (*guhya*) names of the Angels, there transmit our offerings."

95 (*page 138*). See note 79; and cf. *padmapriyā*, characterising Śrī-Lakṣmī, *Śrīsūkta*, 25, where again-*priyā* implies not "choice" but "nature."

96 (*page 141*). A very beautiful description of the creation as reflection is found in *Pañcaviṁśa Brāhmaṇa*, VII, 8, 1, as follows: "The Waters (representing the principle of substance) being ripe unto conception (lit. 'in their season'), Vāyu (that is, the Wind, as physical symbol of spiration, *prâṇa*) moved over their surface. Wherefrom came into being a lovely (*vāma*) thing (that is, the world-picture), there in the Waters Mitra-Varuṇa beheld-themselves-reflected (*paryapaśyat*)." So Genesis, I, 2, The Spirit of God moved over the waters, and St Thomas, *Summ. Theol.*, I, 74, "the Spirit of the Lord signifies the Holy Ghost, Who is said to *move over the water* — that is to say, over what Augustine holds to mean formless matter . . . it is fittingly implied that the Spirit moved over that which was incomplete and unfinished, since that movement is not one of place, but of preëminent power."

The "waters" here and elsewhere in tradition represent the totality of the *possibilities* of being, which from the standpoint of *existence* are in themselves *nothing* (chaos); this "nothing" being "at large" in the First Cause, as explained in note 3. Hence "ex nihilo fit." For the waters in symbolic representation see my *Yakṣas*, II, and in significance, Guénon, *Symbolisme de la Croix*, Ch. XXIV.

97 (*page 142*). With reference, of course, to the three kinds of icons, (1) *dhruva* or *yoga bera* or *mūla vigraha*, permanently established in a shrine, (2) *bhoga mūrti* or *utsava vigraha*, carried in processions, and (3) *dhyāna bera*, mental images used in private devotions.

98 (*page 142*). The *Suprabhedâgama* describes *citra* as *sarvâvayava-saṁpūrṇa-dṛśyaṁ*, and *ardha-citra* as *ardhavâyava-saṁdṛśyaṁ*, respectively "fully visible in all its parts" and "visible as to a half of its parts."

99 (*page 142*). Here evidently *dhātu-rāga*, mineral color, as in *Meghadūta*, p. 102, where the Commentary has *sindūrâdi*, "vermilion, etc.," not *dhātu*, in verse 2 above, as a mineral or some metal other than *loha*, nor *dhātu*, metal, in *Śukranītisāra*, IV, 4, 72 and 153.

100 (*page 143*). Acharya, *Dictionary of Hindu Architecture*, pp. 63, 65, item 5 (out of place); *Mānasāra*, pp. 48, 49.

101 (*page 144*). We find also *pramāṇâbhāsa*, "fallacious proof," *hetvābhāsa*, "logical fallacy," *pratyakṣâbhāsa*, "misleading appearance," *parokṣâbhāsa*, "pseudo-symbolism"; and *pratibhāsa*, "mental reflex" (Stcherbatsky, *Buddhist Logic*, II, 6, n. 2, identifies *pratibhāsa* with *nirbhāsa*, *ābhāsa*, and *pratibimbana*).

102 (*page 145*). See notes 23, 67.

103 (*page 145*). See *Eastern Art*, III (1931), 218, 219.

104 (*page 145*). "Shade and shine," *chāyâtapa*, is taken from *Kaṭha Upaniṣad*, III, 1, and VI, 5, where there is no reference to

any work of art; it occurs also in the *Atthasālinī*, p. 317, in connection with the discussion of *rūpâyatana*, "locus of form" defined as "colored appearance"; "it shines (*nibbhāti*), hence appearance."

Chāyâtapa occurs also in Vasubandhu, *Abhidharmakośa*, III, 39. In all these passages the term bears rather the general meaning "pairs of opposites" than the literal meaning "light and shade"; it is nevertheless actually the immediate equivalent of "chiaroscuro."

105 (*page 146*). B. March, "Linear Perspective in Chinese Painting," *Eastern Art*, III (1931); L. Bachhofer, "Der Raumdarstellung in der chinesischen Malerei, etc." *Münchner Jahrbuch für Bildenden Kunst*, VIII (1931); L. Bachhofer, "Frühindische Historienreliefs," *Ostasiatische Zeitscher.* N. F., VIII (1932), 18; A. Ippel, *Indische Kunst und Triumphalbild* (Leipzig, 1929). The most valuable discussion of this kind is H. Zimmer's "Some Aspects of Time in Indian Art," *Journ. Indian Society of Oriental Art*, I (1933), 30–51.

106 (*page 148*). Sir J. H. Marshall, *Mohenjodaro* (London, 1931), pl. XI; *ASI. AR.* (1917–18), pt. 1, pl. XVI; and *Illustrated London News* (March 24, 1928); Cunningham, *The Stūpa of Bharhut*, 1879, and *M.F.A. Bulletin* 175. Cf. G. Gombaz, "La Loi de Frontalité dans la Sculpture Indienne," *Revue des Arts Asiatiques*, VII, 105.

107 (*page 148*) *Sthānas* are defined in the *Viṣṇudharmottara*, III, 39; *Śilparatna*, Ch. LXIV; Basava Raja, *Śiva Tattva Ratnākara*, VI, 2, 55 ff. See also the general literature on Indian iconography, for example, T. A. C. Rao, *Elements of Hindu Iconography* (Madras, 1914–15). The first five *sthānas* range from (1) frontal or full face to (5) exact profile, intermediate positions being represented by 2, 3, 4. A table of the terms as given in the three sources cited follows:

	Viṣṇudharmottara	*Śilparatna*	*Śiva-Tattva-Ratnākara*
1.	*Ṛju, Ṛjvāgata*	*Ṛju*	*Ṛju, Sammukha*
2.	*Anṛju, Tiryak*	*Ardharju*	*Ardharju*
3.	*Sācikṛta*	*Sācika, Sācigata*	*Sāci*
4.	*Ardhavilocana, Adhyardhâkṣa*	*Dvyardhâkṣi*	*Nyardharju*
5.	*Pārśvagata, Chāyāgata, Bhittika*	*Pārśvagata, Bhittika, Bhittigata*	*Bhittika*
6.	*Parâvṛtta, Gaṇḍaparâvṛtta*		
7.	*Pṛṣṭāgata*		
8.	*Parivṛtta*		
9.	*Samânata*		

108 (*page 149*). See my *History of Indian and Indonesian Art* (1927), pp. 25–27 and fig. 27.

109 (*page 150*). Style is here the datum, appearance, or authority to be investigated. "Those that attempt by means of a (given) authority (that is, from internal evidence) to understand the consciousness (*bodham*) which (itself) produced the authority (*prabodhayantaṁ mānaṁ*) are such great beings as would burn fire itself by means of fuel," Śaṅkarâcārya, *Svâtmanirūpaṇa*, 46.

110 (*page 152*). From the *Sarvadharma-pravṛtti-nirdeśa Sūtra*, cited by Suzuki, *Outlines of Mahayana Buddhism*, p. 381.

111 (*page 156*). See my *Mediaeval Sinhalese Art* (1908), pp. 70–75.

112 (*page 156*). Cf. Pope, G. U., *The Tiruvāçagam* (Oxford, 1900), p. xxxv.

113 (*page 157*). Cf. the *Hermeneia* of Athos, § 445, cited by Fichtner, *Wandmalereien der Athosklöster* (1931), p. 15: "All honor that we pay the image, we refer to the Archetype, namely Him whose image it is. . . . In no wise honor we the colors or

the art, but the archetype in Christ, who is in Heaven. For as Basilius says, the honoring of an image passes over to its prototype." Cf. note 43.

114 (*page 163*). "It is for the advantage (*artha*) of the worshippers (*upāsaka*) (and not by any intrinsic necessity) that the Brahman — whose nature is intelligence (*cin-maya*), beside whom there is no other, who is impartite and incorporeal — is aspectually conceived (*rūpa-kalpanā*)," *Rāmôpaniṣad*, text cited by Bhattacharya, *Indian Images*, p. xvii. That is to say the image, as in the case of any other "arrangement of God," has a merely logical, not an absolute validity. "Worship" (*upāsana*) has been defined as an "intellectual operation (*mānasa-vyāpara*) with respect to the Brahman with attributed-qualities (*saguṇa*)."

115 (*page 168*). Verses cited in the *Triṁśikā* of Vasubandhu; see *Bibliothèque de l'École des Hautes Études*, fasc. 245, 1925, and Lévi, "Matériaux pour l'Étude du Système Vijñaptimātra," *ibid.*, fasc. 260 (Paris, 1932), p. 119.

116 (*page 168*). The stage of partial manifestation is compared to that of the "blooming" of a painting. The term "bloom" or "blossom" (*unmīl*) is used to describe the "coming out" of a painting as the colors are gradually applied (Maheśvarânanda, *Mahârthamañjarī*, p. 44, and my "Further References to Indian Painting," *Artibus Asiae*, p. 127, 1930–1932, item 102).

117 (*page 169*). Cf. my "Hindu Sculpture," in *the league*, vol. V, no. 3 (New York, 1933).

Sanskrit Glossary

Sanskrit Glossary

ābhāsa, "back shining," semblance, reflection; modality (anything regarded as a mode or part of a whole, as painting of sculpture); objectivity; theophany.

abhidhā, denotation; reference.

abhinaya, aesthetic apparatus, means of "registering" (*sūcanā*); especially conventional gestures employed in the dramatic dance (*nṛtya*).

abhi-sambhava, re-becoming, transformation.

abhyāsa, practice, training.

ācārya, a master, one expert in his art.

adhidaivata, from the angelic point of view; *parokṣa*.

adhyātma, from the individual point of view; *pratyakṣa*.

adhyavasāna, introsusceptive, imagist.

āgama, scripture (*śruti*).

āgama-artha-avisaṁvādi, not contradicting the sense of scripture, orthodox, canonical.

āhārya, gotten, acquired, added, adventitious, not innate. *Āhārya-abhinaya*, costume as part of the apparatus of art; *-śobha*, loveliness resulting from adornment.

ākarṣaṇa, attracting, producing; intuition; from *ākṛṣ*.

ākāśa, ether, firmament; immanent space, indefinitely dimensioned, subjective space.

ā-kṛti, image, likeness, outward appearance.

alaṁkāra, ornaments, figures, tropes, associated ideas or images; rhetoric.

a-laukika, not belonging to contingent worlds, supersensuous. Same as *lokôttara*.

ālekhya, painting.

a-mātra, of indefinite measure, undetermined.

ānanda-cin-maya, compounded of delight and reason (characterising *rasâsvādana*, aesthetic experience).

antar-jñeya, known subjectively.

anu-bhāva, means of registration (*sūcanā*) in a work of art; parts or elements of the actual work of art; the physical stimuli to aesthetic reproduction. Cf. *abhinaya*.

anu-kāra, same as *anu-karaṇa*.

anu-karaṇa, "making after," "making in accordance with," imitation; *anukṛti*, *anukāra*.

anu-kārya, the theme "imitated," the model.

anu-kṛti, made in accordance with, "imitation."

anu-māna, inference, deduction, supposition, imputation.

anu-rūpa, like the model, true to nature; analogous.

anu-śīla, devoted application, obedience.

anvita, "caught," conveyed, rendered in a work of art; contrasted with *anyathā*, "off," or "missed."

anyathā, "out," "off," false (in a work of art).

a-parokṣa, not indirect, not symbolic; immediate.

ardha-citra, "half-art," relief (as distinguished from full round sculpture on the one hand and painting on the other).

ardha-likhita, "half-painted," unfinished (distinct from *anyathā*, imperfect, unsuccessful).

artha, meaning, end, interest, use, advantage, motive, purpose, value, determination; just cause or *raison d'être* of a work; "intenzion dell'arte." Cf. *puruṣârtha*.

arthatva, condition of possessing meaning, etc.

āsvāda, tasting (of *rasa*); aesthetic experience.

ātman, self, Self; Universal Man, Brahman.

aupadeśika, acquired by instruction; one who has acquired the appearance of imagination by instruction.

ava-sthāna, condition, emotional situation.

avayava, the separate parts of an organism.

avayava-ānata, attentive to the actual shapes of an object; realistic, "true to Nature."

a-vidyā, non-knowing, relative, empirical, sensible and rational knowledge of plurality.

bāhya, external, objective, empirical.

bhā, to shine forth, appear; in *prati-bhā*.

bhakti, devotion, self-abandonment in love; also used as equivalent to *lakṣaṇā*, connotation; and as a synonym of *dhvani*, content.

bhās, to shine forth; in *ābhāsa*, etc.

bhāva, nature; emotion, sentiment, or mood, as represented in a work of art; the vehicle of *rasa*.

bhavana, "what has come to be," shape, appearance, Nature.

bhāvanā, origination, production, imagination; persistent image, emotional impression surviving in conscious or unconscious memory.

bhoga, fruition, aesthetic appreciation; *āsvāda*.

bhū, to be, become; in *bhāva*, *bhūta*, etc.

bhūta-mātrā, elements of phenomenal being, shape; pictorial (*citra*) factor in art.

bimba, model, subject (presentation, semblance, as contrasted with *prati-bimba*, re-presentation, re-semblance).

buddhi, pure intellect, "the habit of first principles," *prajñā*.

camat-kāra, amazement.

cāru, lovely.

cetanā, sentience, life.

chandas, rhythm.

chāyâtapa, shadow and sunlight, chiaroscuro; pairs of opposites.

cit (*cid-*, *cin-*), mind, intelligence, reason.

citra, representative art (sculpture, relief, painting); picture, pictorial.

citrâbhāsa, "semblance of art," "reflex of sculpture," painting; *ābhāsa*, *ālekhya*.

citra-gata, represented (in a work of art).

citra-kāvya, pictorial or illustrative poetry, the lowest sort, or not poetry at all; cf. "verses for pictures."

citrârdha, same as *ardha-citra*.

citta-vṛtti, fluctuations of the mind, "fugitive emotions and creature images."

daṁsana, grasp (the artist's apprehension of the theme).

darśanīya, worth looking at, good; *quod visum placet*; that which *dṛṣṭi-prītiṁ vidhatte.*

darśita, shown, exhibited, displayed.

deśī, popular, folk (style); contrasted with *mārga*, "high."

deva, *devatā*, angel.

dharaṇa, exclusive attention to a presented idea.

dharma, conduct, morality, law, virtue, function, character, principle, habit, thing.

dhātu, ore; color.

dhvanana, echoing, synonym of *vyañjanā*; cf. *dhvani.*

dhvani, sound, sound*ing*; overtone of meaning, resonance of sense, content (as distinguished from intent); Chinese *yün* (13843).

dhyai, to meditate upon, be intent upon, practice abstract contemplation, visualize. Corresponds to Vedic *dhī.*

dhyāna, undistracted attention, first stage in Yoga praxis; visualization, contemplation of a mental image; Chinese *ch'an*, Japanese *zen.*

dhyāna-yoga, visual contemplative union, realization of formal identity with an inwardly known image.

divya, *daivata*, angelic.

doṣa, any specific fault in a work of art.

dṛś, to see, look, consider, see intuitively; in *dṛśya*, *sādṛśya*, *sadṛśī*, *draṣṭṛ*, etc.

dṛṣṭâdvaita, one who sees without duality, who sees in identity.

dṛṣti-prīti, delight of the eyes.

dṛśya, visible, the phenomenal universe.

gamana, motion, movement.

graha, seizer, apprehender, sense-instrument.

grahaṇa, "seizing," comprehension, understanding of anything.

grāhya, seizable, able to be comprehended.

guha, gupta, guhya, hidden, occult, unseen; transcendental.
guṇa, any specific merit in a work of art. Also factor, quality or qualification in the phenomenal universe, viz. *sattva-guṇa,* purity, *rajo-guṇa,* action, expansion, continuation, and *tamo-guṇa,* inertia, resistance.

haraṇa, plagiarism.
harṣa, delight.
hṛd, hṛdaya, heart, the entire being (sensible and intelligent); soul; Self, Brahman.

itihāsa, narrative, history.

jagac-citra, world picture, vision of the Universe apart from time.
jīva, jīvâtman, individual, self, soul.
jīvan-mukta, one who has attained spiritual freedom, but is still manifest in human form.

kailāsa-bhāvanā, made after the heavenly pattern.
kalā, art, any art or accomplishment depending on skill. Art as avocation. The *bāhya-kalās* (external arts, or practical arts) are usually listed as sixty-four in number, some being identical with the vocational *śilpas*; there are also sixty-four *kāma-* or *abhyantara,* "arts of love," or "intimate arts."
kāma, pleasure of any kind, specific or natural pleasure, especially in love.
kānti, loveliness (of the subject, esp. in a portrait).
kāraka, maker, creator.
kāraṇa, act, action, cause; formal gesture or position in dancing.
karma, making (with reference to man's handiwork, *factibile*); also conduct (with reference to man's deeds, *agibile*); office, celebration, ritual.
kārya, to be made, *factibile.*
kārayitṛ, creative.
kauśala, skill, expertness, virtuosity, facility; when as in Buddhist usage there is a moral coloring, the idea of "convenience" is also present.

kautūhala, interest in, appreciation of, a work of art.

kavi, in the Vedas, Poetic Genius (personified) a designation of the Sun, as "revealer"; later, "poet," artist.

kavitva, artistry; *-dāyin*, artistic.

kāvya, poetry (prose or verse); "literature" as distinct from *śruti* and *itihāsa*, *śāstras*, etc. By extension, "art" as an abstract concept. *Kavitva-dāyin*, "artistic."

kāvya-śarīra, the body of poetry (consisting of sound, sense and ornaments); the work of art as a physical entity, as distinguished from its soul, or content, *ātman*.

kṛ, to do, make; in *karma*, *karaṇa*, *kārya*, etc.

kṛṣ, to attract, draw, delineate, display; in *ākarṣaṇa*, etc.

kṛta, made, well and truly made.

kṛtârtha, purpose or end of the work to be done.

kha, space; *ākāśa*.

kratv-artha, the good of the work to be done.

lakṣaṇa, characteristic lineament, iconographic requirement, sign, symbol, attribute.

lakṣaṇā, connotation.

lāvaṇya, "salt," charm, "it" (in a feminine subject).

laya, rest, cessation, resolution.

likh, to draw, paint; in *ālekhya*, etc.

līlā, play, unmotivated manifestation.

loka, world, sphere, universe; the conditioned world, including heaven, in part.

loka-vṛtta, "local motions," phenomena; "Nature" (*ens naturata*).

lokôttara, supersensual (rather than "supernatural").

mā, to measure; in *māna*(1), *pramāṇa*, *nirmāṇa*, *pratimā*, *nirmā*, *mātrā*.

mādhurya, sweetness, equanimity, grace, facility.

māna (1), (from root *mā*), measure, canon of proportion.

māna (2), (from root *man*), pride, egoism, ideology. Cf. "mental" (rational) as used by Blake.

manas, intellect, mind, reason; *divyacakṣu* (*Chāndogya Up.*, VIII, 12, 5).

manohara, delighting the mind or heart; affective, seductive.

mantra, incantation, enchantment (e.g., verses of the *Ṛg Veda*, and canonical prescriptions of the *Śilpa Śāstras*, known as *dhyāna mantras*).

mānuṣa, human.

mārga, high (style): same as *rīti*. Contrasted or "stylistic" or "sophisticated" with *deśī*, "folk," "naïve."

mātrā, measure, dimension, principle.

māyā, creative power; magic; *natura naturans*.

mokṣa, liberation, spiritual freedom, realization (not "attainment") of perfection.

mūrta, formal, in a likeness; contrasted with *a-mūrta*, imageleso, transcending form.

mūrti, form, image, likeness.

naisargika, innate, natural; *sahaja*.

nāma, name, idea, form; means of conventional discrimination.

nāma-rūpa, name and aspect, words and images, the means of conventional discrimination, that by which the contingent universe is known.

natônnata, relief, relievo, in a painting.

nāya, traditional authority, prescription.

netrâmṛta, elixir of the eyes, that which delights the eye.

nimnônnata, same as *natônnata*.

nirmā, with *citram*, to paint; with *kośam*, to compose, write.

nirmāṇa, making, creating, manifestation.

nirmāṇa-kāraka, maker, creator; God.

nirvāha, bare statement of fact, narration.

niyama, ascertained rule.

nṛtya, dramatic dance, art-dance, nautch; dance giving expression to *rasa* and *bhāva*.

padminī, "lotus lady," one of the four types of women.

paramârtha, ultimate significance; essence, Brahman, *ātman*.

pāramârthika, with respect to ultimate significance, transcendental, absolute.

parāvṛtti, transformation, transubstantiation, anagogy.

pari-, prefix = *per*.

pari-draṣṭṛ, over-seer, witness, God.

pari-haraṇa, flagrant plagiarism.

paṭa, canvas, painting.

pradeśa, landscape, area.

pra-harṣa, great delight.

pra-hṛṣṭa, delighted (by a work of art).

prajñā, discrimination, wisdom, pure intellect, First Principle, Brahman.

prajñā-mātrā, elements of intelligence or discrimination; formal elements in art.

prajñāna-ghana, exemplary understanding.

pramāṇa, as principle, ideal symmetry, aesthetic conscience, "correction du savoir faire"; as canon, same as *māna*.

pramātṛ, judge, critic, one possessed of a subjective criterion, or aesthetic standard (*pramāṇa*).

pra-muda, delight, great delight; same as *praharṣa*.

prâṇa, spiration, life-breath, *pneuma*; Chinese *ch'i*; life as procession, emanation. In the plural, the distinct life breaths in the individual species.

prati-, a prefix: toward, against, counter-.

prati-bhā, vision, imagination, poetic faculty.

prati-bimba, representation; *-vat*, *quā* representation.

pratīka, symbol.

prati-kṛti, portrait; *ākṛti*, *ākara*.

pratimā, image, likeness; *-kāraka*, imager.

pratīti, self-intelligibility, clear intuition or manifestation (of *rasa*).

prati-vihita, determined ($\sqrt{dh\bar{a}}$).

pratyakṣa, "before the eye," evident, objective, perceptible; empirical observation; like the model, true to Nature; semiotic. Cf. *parokṣa*.

prayojana, use, application, purpose, intent, theme; cf. *artha*.

pūjā, office, ritual; *pūjya*, to be worshipped.

puruṣa, person, personality. Distinguished from *jīva*, individual.

puruṣârtha, value, the meaning or purpose of life; the Four Ends of Life, viz. *dharma*, *artha*, *kāma*, *mokṣa*. The advantage to be derived from the accomplished work, as distinguished from *kratvartha*, the good of the work to be done.

ramaṇīyatā, beauty in a work of art, especially as seen in disinterested contemplation.

ramya, lovely, truly lovely, beautiful.

raṅga, color.

rasa, flavor, savor, quintessence; the substance of aesthetic experience, knowable only in the activity of tasting, *rasâsvādana*.

rasâsvādana, tasting of *rasa*, aesthetic experience.

rasâtmaka, having *rasa* as its soul.

rasavat, possessing *rasa*, said of a work of art, by imputation or projection.

rasâyana, elixir for the eyes, said of a work of art as good to see.

rasika, one competent to the tasting of *rasa*, true critic.

rekhā, line, outline, drawing.

rekhā-śuddhi, purity of line.

rīti, style, diction, composition, manner.

ruci, taste, preference (not to be confused with *rasa*).

rūpa, shape, natural shape, semblance, color, loveliness; image, effigy, likeness; symbol, ideal form; means of conventional discrimination (see *nāma-rūpa*). (Cf. *vi-rūpa*, having two forms, various, altered, deformed, ugly; and *a-rūpa*, not formed, transcendental.)

rūpa-kāra, imager (maker of images).

rūpa-sobhā, represented beauty.

rūpya, beautiful, shapely; formal.

rutârtha, sound and sense.

śabda, sound, word: Logos.

śabdârtha, same as *rutârtha*.

sādhana, any means employed in worship; a canonical prescription, *dhyāna mantra*.

sā-dhāraṇya, "having a common support"; ideal sympathy, disinterested *Ein-* or *Mitfühlung*.

sādhu, what is good or right in a work of art (opposite of *anyathā*); as an exclamation, "Well done."

sa-dṛśa, *sa-dṛśī*, like in appearance, sensibly resembling.

sā-dṛśya, concomitance of formal and pictorial elements, conformity, *consonantia*: Chinese *ch'ou* (2508), "answering to," "in response."

sahaja, innate, connatural; spontaneous, spontaneity; "willingly but not from will, naturally but not from nature." Contrasted with *aupadeśika*, and *āhārya*.

sā-hitya, concomitance of sound and sense, word and meaning: *consonantia*.

sa-hṛdaya, "having a heart," imaginatively or spiritually gifted; *rasika*.

sâkṣāt, present to the eye, *pratyakṣa*.

śakti, power, genius.

sālakṣya, having like features, similarity, common denotation.

saṁkalpa, concept, conception, imagining, mental formulation.

saṁketa, convention.

saṁketita, conventional.

saṁskṛ, to con-struct, integrate; *saṁskṛta*, the arti-ficial, constructed, integrated language, Sanskrit.

saṁtoṣa, satisfaction (derived from a work of art).

saṁvādi, agreeing with, conformable to the model or prescription.

saṁvyavahārika, worldly, practical.

sārasvata, inspired by or worthy of Sarasvatī.

śarīra, body, substance: the material body of a work of art, as composed of sounds, tangible forms, etc.; the tangible embodiment of intuition-expression.

sārūpya, co-aspectuality, con-formation, coördination, correspondence; cf. *sādṛśya*.

śāstra, a scripture or treatise written by a sage; traditional authority (*smṛti*) as distinguished from revelation (*śruti*).

śāstra-māna, canonical, according to traditional authority.

sat (*sad-*), true, real.

sattva, purity, simplicity; quality of essence, being in itself; the first of the three *guṇas*.

sattva-bhāva, any natural expression of emotion, as represented in art.

satya, true, real, essential; sacred, hieratic (painting).

sa-varṇa, double, substitute.

śilpa (Pali *sippa*) art, any art or work of art, the practice of art, skill of art, art as vocation, taught by a master (*ācārya*). *Śilpa-jīvin*, one who lives by his art, a professional. Cf. *kalā*.

śithila, slack, not intense; with *-samādhi*, imperfect concentration of the artist (in medicine, post coitum lassitude).

śliṣṭatva, habitus, wont, facility, knack.

smṛti, "remembered"; tradition, authority, cf. *śāstra*. Also "memory," but in a bad sense, as nostalgia, or sentimentality, not "recollection."

śravaṇīya, worth listening to, good (of music, etc.).

śṛṅgāra, the erotic, most important of the separate *rasas*.

śruti, heard, audition, "revelation," immediate authority, scripture; the Vedas.

sthāna, station, field; pose.

sthāyi, established, stable, permanent. With *-bhāva*, permanent mood, constant motif of a work of art.

sthūla, gross (material, as opposed to mental).

sūcanā, registering (as in cinema parlance).

sūkṣma, subtle (mental, as opposed to physical).

su-kṛta, well and truly made (of the world, as God's art); perfect. See list, n. 107.

suṣṭhu, excellent (in praise of a work of art).

sva, self, own.

sva-bhāva, own-being, essential nature, inwardness.
sva-dharma, vocation, calling, specific function.
sva-prakāśa, self-illuminated, self-manifesting (*rasa*, or Brahman), limpid.
sva-rūpa, own form, very form; intrinsic aspect; *svâkāra*.

tad-ākāratā, con-formation, coordination.
tad-anurūpa, according to the model, like, true to nature.
tad-ātmya, having the same self as.
tat lagnaṁ hṛd, the seductive, intriguing.
tād-rūpya, of like form, like.
takṣ, to hew (wood; or, metaphorically, thought).
tāla, *tāla-māna*, measure, canon of proportion.
tātparya-artha, meaning or significance of the whole phrase or work of art, as distinct from that of its separate parts or elements.

unmīl, to bloom (said of a painting while being colored).
upacāra, metaphor, analogy.
upāsaka, worshipper.
upāsana, worship.
utsāha, "effort"; the spiritual energy exerted in aesthetic reproduction.

vāc (*vāk-*, *vāg-*), voice (as function); speech (as discrimination, exterior word); interior word, Logos; wisdom.
vaidagdhya, skill.
vākya, word, phrase; expression.
vāraṇa, wall, barrier, enclosure; hindrance (e. g. prejudice, interest, appetite).
varṇa, color, sound; scale, palette.
varṇaṇīya, to be depicted or expressed; praiseworthy (theme).
varṇikā-bhaṅga, distribution of color.
vartanā, Pali *vattana*, shading, that is, plastic modelling, in painting.
vartikā, brush.

vāsanā, latent memory of past experience, hence the potentiality of impartial sensibility, fancy, *Einfühlung*. In the bad sense, emotional associations and attachments; power of habit.

vastu, theme, subject.

vi-bhāva, physical stimulant to aesthetic reproduction; the parts of the work of art, aesthetic surfaces.

vicitra, variegated, romantic.

vidyā, gnosis, un-knowing, the immediate knowledge (realization) of unity, absolute truth; = *prajñā*, *jñāna*.

vikalpa, rational knowledge.

vilekhana, same as *ālekhya*, painting.

visaṁvādi, not agreeing (with the model or prescription).

viśeṣa-jña, of varied knowledge, connoisseur.

vivāda-nirṇaya, judgment, discrimination.

vyabhicāri, fugitive, transient (with *-bhāva*, transient mood or emotion, as contrasted with *sthāyi-bhāva*).

vyāhṛti, utterance, Spoken Word.

vyaṅgyārtha, suggested meaning, content, significance (as distinguished from denotation and connotation).

vyañjanā, suggestive power of an expression.

vyavahārika, worldly, empirical, sensational.

vyutpatti, explicit meaning, conceptual part of art; scholarship.

yajña, sacrificial office.

yantra, "device," "machine"; geometrical representation of a deity.

yoga, lit. "union," "yoking"; skill in action (*Bhagavad Gītā*, II, 50).

yogyā, application, study, practice.

yuj (in *yoga*, *prayojana*, etc.), to yoke, apply, exert, control.

yukta, yoked, joined to, embodying, united, at-oned.

yukti, skill, accomplishment, acquired facility.

List of Chinese Characters

List of Chinese Characters*

ch'an (Giles, 348), Sanskrit *dhyāna*, Japanese *zen.*

chêng (Giles, 720), used by Hsüan Tsang to render *pramāṇa.*

ch'i (Giles, 991), extraordinary, marvellous, surprising.

ch'i (Giles, 1064), spirit, spiration, breath, life. Sanskrit *prâṇa*, Greek *pneuma*, Arabic *rūḥ*. The procession of *ch'i* is from Heaven and Earth, the primary modalities of the First Principle (Tao), hence *ch'i* is rightly used to render "Holy Ghost."

ch'iao (Giles, 1411), clever, skilful, artful.

chih (Giles, 1783), to know, knowledge; conscience.

ch'ou (Giles, 2508), reciprocity; used by Hsüan Tsang to render *sādṛśya.*

ch'uan (Giles, 2740), handed down, transmitted; tradition. "What he gets by his mind (*shin*) he transmits by his hand" (said of the painter).

fu (Giles, 3632), to lay on color.

hsin (Giles, 4562), heart, mind, spirit. Cf. Sanskrit *hṛdaya.*

hsing (Giles, 4617), natural shape; objective; represented shape. Skr. *rūpa.*

i (Giles, 5536), supersensual perfection of the sage; genius; spontaneity. Cf. *shên* and Skr. *śakti sahaja.*

i (Giles, 5367), idea, mind, intuition, meaning, end. Contrasted with *hsing*. Cf. Sanskrit *artha*, *nāma*, and *pramāṇa.*

i ch'ü (Giles, 5367, 3120) operation of the mind; movement of the idea; significance, thought. Dante's "intenzion dell' arte," *Paradiso*, 1, 127.

liang (Giles, 7015), measure, standard. (Sanskrit *pramāṇa*?)

* The numbers of the characters are those of Giles's *Chinese-English Dictionary*, where they can easily be found, and the shades of meaning considered.

miao (Giles, 7857), profound, mysterious, wonderful.

nêng (Giles, 8184), ability, skill, accomplishment, virtuosity. Same as *ch'iao*.

san p'in (Giles, 9552, 9273), The three kinds of painting, ***shên, miao, nêng***.

shên (Giles, 9819), angel, angelic, divine spirit, soul, God; Skr. *deva*. "The inscrutable operation of Yin and Yang is called *shên*": "to paint a portrait (*fu shên*)": "to give expression (*shên*) to the very part left undelineated." *Ching* (2133) ***shên***, "very soul," "true self."

ssŭ (Giles, 10289), likeness, resemblance, imitation.

wu (Giles, 12777), object, Nature; *viṣaya-rūpatā*.

yün (Giles, 13817), operation, revolution; Pacioli's *movimenti*.

yün (Giles, 13843), resonance, reverberation, content. Cf. Sanskrit *dhvani*.

Bibliography

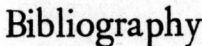

Bibliography

1. European Languages

ACHARYA, P. K. *Dictionary of Hindu Architecture.* Oxford, n.d.[1]

—— *A Summary of the Mānasāra.* Leiden, 1918.[1]

—— *Indian Architecture according to the Mānasāra-Śilpaśāstra.* Oxford, n.d.[1]

ANAND, M. R. *The Hindu View of Art.* London, 1933.

ANESAKI, M. *Buddhist Art in Its Relation to Buddhist Ideals.* Boston, 1911; 2nd ed., 1915.

ARAVAMUTHAN, T. G. *Portrait Sculpture in South India.* London, 1931.

ASANGA. *Mahāyāna Sūtrâlaṁkāra.* Translated by Sylvain Lévi. Paris, 1911.

BACHHOFER, L. "Die Raumdarstellung in der chinesischen Malerei," *Münchner Jahrbuch für bildenden Kunst*, VIII, 1931.

—— "Frühindische Historienreliefs," *Ostas. Zeitschrift*, N. F., VIII, 1932.

BANERJEA, J. N. *Pratimālakṣaṇam.* Edited and translated, Calcutta, 1932.[1]

BARNETT, L. D. *The Lord's Song* (*Bhagavad Gītā*), Temple Classics.

—— *Antagaḍa Dasāo.* London, 1907.

BHATTACHARYA, B. C. *Indian Images.* Calcutta, 1921.

BHATTACHARYYA, B. *Buddhist Iconography.* Oxford, 1924.

—— *Buddhist Esoterism.* Oxford, 1932. (Ch. XI.)

BINYON, L. *Painting in the Far East*, 3rd ed. London, 1923.

—— *The Flight of the Dragon* (various editions).

BOAS, F. *Primitive Art.* Oslo, 1927.

[1] *Śilpa Śāstras.*

BÖHME, J. *Mysterium Pansophicum*. Translated by J. R. Earle. New York, 1920.

BOSE, N. K. *Canons of Orissan Architecture*. Calcutta, 1933.[1]

BOSE, P. N. *Principles of Indian Śilpaśāstra*. Punjab Oriental Series, XI. Lahore, 1926.

—— *Pratimā-Māna-Lakṣaṇam*. Punjab Oriental Series, XVIII. Lahore, 1929.

CHATTERJI, J. C. *Kashmir Shaivism*. 1914.

COOMARASWAMY, A. K. "Teaching of Drawing in Ceylon," *Ceylon National Review*, December, 1906 (also in *Mediaeval Sinhalese Art*, Broad Campden, 1908).

—— *Mediaeval Sinhalese Art*. Broad Campden, 1908.

—— *The Indian Craftsman*. London, 1909.

—— "That Beauty is a State," *Burlington Magazine*, April, 1915.

—— *Rajput Painting*. Oxford, 1916.

—— *The Dance of Śiva*. New York, 1918.

—— *Citra-lakṣaṇa* (*Śilparatna*, Ch. 64). Sir Ashutosh Mukerjee Memorial Volume. Patnā, 1926–28.

—— "Nāgara Painting," *Rūpam*, Nos. 37, 40, 1929.

—— "An Early Passage on Indian Painting," *Eastern Art*, III, 1931.

—— "One Hundred References to Indian Painting," *Artibus Asiae*, 1930–32, pp. 41–57, and "Further References," pp. 126–129.

—— "Introduction to the Art of Eastern Asia," *Open Court*, March, 1932 (partly identical with the present text).

—— Viṣṇudharmottara (III), 41, *JAOS*., LII, 1932.[1]

—— "The Technique and Theory of Indian Painting," *Technical Studies in the Field of the Fine Arts*, III, 1934.

—— "Hindu Sculpture," *the league*, V. New York, 1933.

—— *Elements of Buddhist Symbolism*. Cambridge, 1934.[2]

—— *A New Approach to the Vedas*. London, 1934.[2]

[1] *Śilpa Śāstras*. [2] In Press.

COOMARASWAMY, A. K. "Mediaeval Aesthetic. I. Dionysius the Pseudo-Areopagite, and Ulrich Engelberti of Strasburg," *Art Bulletin*, March, 1935.

COOMARASWAMY, A. K., and DUGGIRALA, G. K. *The Mirror of Gesture.* Cambridge, 1917.

CROCE, B. "The Breviary of Aesthetic," *Rice Institute Pamphlet*, 11, 1915.

DANDOY, J., *L'Ontologie du Vedānta.* Paris, 1932.

DAS GUPTA. *History of Indian Philosophy.* Cambridge, Eng., 1922, 1932.

DE, SUSHIL K. *Sanskrit Poetics*, 2 vols. London, 1923, 1925.

DEUSSEN, P. *Philosophy of the Upanishads.* Edinburgh, 1906.

DUTT, M. N. *Dissertation on Painting.* Calcutta, 1922.[1]

DVOŘAK, M. *Kunstgeschichte als Geistesgeschichte, Studien zur abendländischen Kunstentwicklung.* München, 1924.

EDGERTON, F. *Vikrama's Adventures.* Translation of the *Vikramacarita.* Harvard Oriental Series, XXXVI. Cambridge, 1926.

EVANS, C. de B. *Meister Eckhart.* London, 1924.

FONSEKA, L. DE. *On the Truth of Decorative Art.* London, 1913.

FOX-STRANGWAYS. *The Music of Hindustan.* Oxford, 1914.

FOUCHER, A. *L'Iconographie bouddhique de l'Inde.* Paris, 1900, 1905.

GILES, H. A. *Chuang Tzŭ.* London, 1889.

GILL, E. *Art-Nonsense.* London, 1929.

GOMBAZ, G. "La Loi de Frontalité dans le Sculpture indienne," *Revue des Arts asiatiques*, VII, 1931–32.

GROSLIER, G. "Notes sur la Psychologie de l'Artisan cambodgien," *Arts et Archéologie khmèrs*, I.

—— "Le Fin d'un Art," *Revue des Arts asiatiques*, V.

GUÉNON, R. *L'Homme et son Devenir selon le Vedanta.* Paris, 1925.

—— *Introduction générale à l'Étude des Doctrines hindoues.* Paris, 1932.

[1] Not seen by the author.

Guénon, R. *La Symbolisme de la Croix*. Paris, 1931.

Havell, E. B. *Ideals of Indian Art*. London, 1911.

Hearn, L. *Japan, an Interpretation*. New York, 1905.

Hemacandra. *Triṣaṣṭiśalākāpuruṣacaritra*. Translated by H. M. Johnson, I. Baroda, 1931.

Hirn, Yrjö. *The Origins of Art*. London, 1900.

Hume, R. E. *The Thirteen Principal Upanishads*, 2nd ed. Oxford, 1931.

Ippel, A. *Indische Kunst und Triumphalbild*. Leipzig, 1929.

Jacovleff, A., and Tchou-Kia-Kien. *The Chinese Theatre*. London, 1922.

Jinavaravamsa, P. C. "Notes on Siamese Arts and Crafts," *Ceylon National Review*, No. 4, July, 1907.

Jitta-Zadoks. *Ancestral Portraiture in Rome*. Amsterdam, 1932.

Jung, C. G. *Psychological Types*. London, 1926.

Kakuzo, O. *The Ideals of the East*. New York, 1904.

—— *The Book of Tea*. New York, 1906.

Keith, A.B. *History of Sanskrit Literature*. Oxford, 1928.

—— *Aitareya and Kauṣītaki Brāhmaṇas*. Harvard Oriental Series, XXV, 1920.

—— *Buddhist Philosophy*. Oxford, 1923.

Kramrisch, S. *The Vishṇudharmottara*, 2nd ed. Calcutta, 1928.[1]

—— "Landschaft, Tier, und geometrisches Muster in der indischen Kunst." *Josef Strzygowski Festschrift*. Klagenfurt, 1932.

—— *Indian Sculpture*. Calcutta, 1933.

Lalou, M. *L'Iconographie des Étoffes peints (paṭa) dans le Mañjuśrīmulakalpa*. Buddhica, VI. Paris, 1930.

Laufer, B. *Dokumente der indischen Kunst: I, Das Citralakṣaṇa*. Leipzig, 1913.[1]

Lelyveld, Th. B van. *La Danse dans le Théâtre javanais*. Paris, 1931.

Lévi, S. *Matériaux pour l'Étude du Système Vijñaptimātra*. Paris, 1932.

[1] *Śilpa-Śāstra.*

MARCH, B. "Linear Perspective in Chinese Painting," *Eastern Art*, III, 1931.
MARITAIN, J. *Art and Scholasticism*. London, 1930.
—— *Introduction to Philosophy*. London, 1932.
MARSHALL, SIR J. H. *Mohenjodaro*. London, 1931.
MASSON-OURSEL. *Esquisse d'une Histoire de la Philosophie indienne*, esp. pp. 156, 288. Paris, 1923.
—— "Une Connexion dans l'Ésthétique et la Philosophie de l'Inde," *Rev. des Arts asiatiques*, II, 1925 (transl. in *Rūpam*, 27/28, 1926).
——, WILMAN-GRABOWSKA, H. de, and Stern, P., *L'Inde antique et la Civilisation indienne*. Paris, 1933. (Pt. IV, La vie esthétique.)
MEERWARTH, A. "Les Kathakalis du Malabar." *Journal Asiatique*, Paris, CCIX, Oct.–Dec., 1926.
MUKERJI, S. C. *Le Rasa, Essai sur l'Esthétique indienne*. Paris, 1928.
OLDENBERG, H. "Vedic Words for 'Beautiful' and 'Beauty' and the Vedic Sense of the Beautiful," *Rūpam*, No. 32, 1928.
PETRUCCI, R. *Encyclopédie de la Peinture chinoise*. Paris, 1918.
—— *La Philosophie de la Nature dans l'Art d'Extrême-Orient*. Paris, n.d.
PODUVAL, R. V. *The Art of Kathākali*. Trivandrum, 1933.
POPE, G. U. *The Tiruvāçagam*. Oxford, 1900.
RAM RAZ. *Essay on the Architecture of the Hindus*. London, 1834.
RAO, T. A. G. *Elements of Hindu Iconography*. Madras, 1914, 1916.[1]
—— *Tālamāna or Iconometry*. Memoirs of the Archaeological Survey of India, III. Calcutta, 1920.
REGNAUD, P. *La Rhêtorique sanskrite*. Paris, 1884.
SARKAR, B. K. *The Śukranīti*. Sacred Books of the Hindus, XII. Allahābād, 1914.
ŚAUNAKA. *Bṛhad Devatā*. Translated by A. A. Macdonell. Harvard Oriental Series, VI. Cambridge, 1904.

[1] *Śilpa-Śāstra*.

SCHLOSSER, J. *Die Kunstliteratur.* Vienna, 1924.

SIRÉN, O. *A History of Early Chinese Painting.* London, 1933.

STCHERBATSKY, TH. *Buddhist Logic.* Leningrad, 1930, 1932.

STRZYGOWSKI, J. *Asiatische Miniaturmalerei, im Anschluss an Wesen und Werden der Mogulmalerei.* Klagenfurt, 1933.

SUZUKI, D. T. *Essays in Zen Buddhism.* London, 1927–

—— *Outlines of Mahayana Buddhism.* London, 1907.

—— *The Laṅkâvatāra Sūtra.* London, 1932.

TAGORE, A., *L'Alpona.* Paris, 1921.

—— *Art et Anatomie hindoue.* Paris, 1921.

—— *Sadanga.* Paris, 1922.

TAGORE, R. *Poems of Kabir* (various editions).

TAKI, S. *Three Essays in Oriental Painting.* London, 1910.

—— *Japanese Fine Arts.* Tokio, 1931.

THOMAS AQUINAS, St. *Summa Theologica.*

VASUBANDHU. *Abhidharmakośa.* Translated by L. de la Vallée Poussin. Louvain, 1923–1931.

VENKATA, RAO, M. A. "Aesthetics in India," *Aryan Path,* IV, 715–720, 1933.

VENKATASSUBBIAH, A. *The Kalās.* Madras, 1911.

VENKATASUBBIAH, A., and MÜLLER, E. The Kalās, *JRAS.*, 1914.

VIŚVANATHA. *Sāhitya Darpaṇa.* Translated as *The Mirror of Composition,* by Premadasa Mitra. Calcutta, 1875.

WALEY, A. *The Nō Plays of Japan.* London, 1921.

—— *Zen Buddhism in its Relation to Art.* London, 1922.

—— *An Introduction to the Study of Chinese Painting.* London, 1923.

—— *The Tale of Genji,* 6 vols. London, 1925–33.

WOODROFFE, SIR J. *The Garland of Letters.* London, 1922.

—— "Psychology of Hindu Religious Ritual," *Indian Art and Letters,* I, 1925.

—— "The Indian Magna Mater," *ibid.*, II, 1926.

WULF, M. DE. *Études historiques sur l'Ésthetique de St. Thomas d'Aquin.* Löwen, 1896.[1]

[1] Not seen by the author.

ZIMMER, H. *Kunstform und Yoga im indischen Kultbild*. Berlin, 1926.

—— "Some Aspects of Time in Indian Art," *Journ. Indian Society of Oriental Art*, I, 1933, pp. 30–51.

2. SANSKRIT WORKS

Aitareya Brāhmaṇa. Ed. Sāmaśramī, Bibliotheca Indica, Calcutta, 1895, 1896.

Asaṅga, *Mahāyāna Sūtrâlaṁkāra*. Ed. Sylvain Lévi, Paris, 1925.

Basava Rāja, *Śiva Tattva Ratnākara*. Ed. B. R. Rao and P. S. Sastriar, Madras, 1927. (See *Kalolla* VI, *Taraṅga* 2.)

Bhagavad Gītā. Various editions.

Bharata, *Nāṭya Śāstra*. Ed. M. Ramakrishna Kavi, Gaekwar's Oriental Series, XXXVI (Vol. I), Baroda, 1926.

Bhāsa, *Dūtavākya*. Gaṇapati Śāstri's ed., Trivandrum, 1925.

—— *Pratimānāṭaka*. Paranjape's ed., Poona, 1927.

—— *Pratijñāyaugandhārāyaṇa*. Gaṇapati Śāstri's ed., Trivandrum, 1920.

—— *Svapnavāsavadatta*. Gaṇapati Śāstri's ed., Trivandrum, 1926.

Bhavabhūti, *Uttara-Rāma-carita*. Belvalkar's ed., Poona, 1921.

Bhojadeva, *Samarâṅgaṇasūtradhāra*. Ed. T. Gaṇapati Śāstri, Gaekwar's Oriental Series, XXV, Baroda, 1924.[1]

—— *Yukti-Kalpataru*. Candra Śāstri's ed., Calcutta, 1917.[1]

Bṛhad Devatā. Ed. Macdonell, Harvard Oriental Series, V, Cambridge, 1904.

Citralakṣaṇa. (1) See Laufer, in Bibliography 1, above. (2) Ch. 64 of the *Śilparatna*, *q.v.*[1]

Daṇḍin, *Daśakumāracarita*. Ed. Wilson, London, 1846.

Dhanaṁjaya, *Daśarūpa*. Text and translation, ed. Haas, New York, 1912.

Divyâvadāna. Ed. Cowell, E. B., and Neil, R. A., Cambridge, Eng., 1888.

[1] *Śilpa Śāstras*.

Harṣa, *Priyadarśikā*. Ed. and tr. by Nariman and Ogden, Columbia University Indo-Iranian Series, X, New York, 1923.

Hemacandra, *Triṣaṣṭiśalākāpuruṣacaritra* (*Ādīśvaracaritra*). Bhavnagar, 1905.

Jaiminīya Upaniṣad Brāhmaṇa. Ed. and tr. Oertel, *JAOS*., XVI, New Haven, 1894.

Kālidāsa, *Śakuntalā*. (1) Pischel's ed., Harvard Oriental Series, XVI, Cambridge, 1922, (2) Kale's ed. (*Abhijñāna-śakuntalam*), Bombay, 1913.

—— *Vikramôrvaśī*. Kale's 6th ed., Bombay, 1922.

—— *Kumārasambhava*. Kale's 5th ed., Bombay, 1923.

—— *Mālavikâgnimitra*. Paranjape's ed., Poona, 1918.

—— *Raghuvaṁśa*. Nandargikar's 3rd ed., Bombay, 1897.

Kāma Sūtra. Kāshī Sanskrit Series, XXIX, Benares, 1929 (with Yaśodhara's commentary).

Kāśyapaśilpam. Anandâśrama Skr. Series, XCV, 1926.[1]

Lalita Vistara. Ed. Lefmann, Halle, 1902.

Laṅkâvatāra Sūtra. Nanjō's ed. Tokyō, 1923.

Mayamuni, *Mayamata*. Ed. T. Gaṇapati Śāstri, Trivandrum Skr. Series, LXV, Trivandrum, 1919.[1]

Pañcaviṁśa Brāhmaṇa. Vedântavāgīśa's ed., Bibliotheca Indica, Calcutta, 1870, 1874.

Prakāśânanda, *Siddhântamuktāvalī*. Reprint from *The Pandit*. Benares, 1898.

Pratimā-Māna-Lakṣaṇam. Ed. P. N. Bose, Punjab Oriental Series, XVIII, Lahore, 1929.[1]

Rājaśekhara, *Karpūramañjarī*. Ed. and tr. by Konow and Lanman, Harvard Oriental Series, IV, Cambridge, 1901.

—— *Kāvyamīmāṁsā*. Gaekwar's Oriental Series, Baroda, 1924.

Ṛg Veda Saṁhitā. Ed. Max Müller. London, 1849–1874.

Saddharma Puṇḍarīka. Kern and Nanjio's ed., Bibliotheca Buddhica, St. Petersburg, 1912.

Sādhanamālā. Ed. B. Bhattacharyya, Gaekwar's Oriental Series, XXVI, XLI, Baroda, 1925, 1928.[1]

[1] *Śilpa Śāstras*.

Śaṅkarâcārya: *Svâtmanirūpaṇa*; *Śataślokī*. Minor Works of Shankaracharya. Ed. H. R. Bhagavat, Poona, 1925.
—— *Brahmasūtra-bhāṣya*. Ed. Paṅśikar, 2nd ed., Bombay, 1927.
Śatapatha Brāhmaṇa. Ed. Sāmaśramī, Bibliotheca Indica, Calcutta, 1907–1911.
Śrī Kumāra, *Śilparatna*. Ed. T. Gaṇapati Śāstri, Trivandrum Skr. Series, LXXV, XCVIII, Trivandrum, 1922, 1929.[1]
Śūdraka, *Mṛcchakaṭika*. Parab's 5th ed., Bombay, 1922.
Śukrâcārya, *Śukranītisāra*. Vidyāsagara's ed., Calcutta, 1890.
Upaniṣads. Various editions.
Vasubandhu, *Triṁśikā*. Ed. Sylvain Lévi, Paris, 1925.
—— *Viṁśatikā*. Ed. Sylvain Lévi, Paris, 1925.
Viṣṇudharmottara. Ed. Pandit Mādhavaprasād, Bombay, 1911.
Viśvanātha, *Sāhitya Darpaṇa*. Kane's ed., Bombay, 1923.
Yāska, *Nighaṇṭu and Nirukta*. Ed. Sarup, Lahore, 1927.

3. Pali and Prakrit

Āyāraṁga Sutta. Ed. Jacobi, Pali Text Soc., London, 1882.
Buddhaghoṣa, *Atthasālinī*. Ed. E. Müller, Pali Text Soc., London, 1897.
Cūḷavaṁsa. Ed. Geiger, Pali Text Soc., London, 1925, 1927.
Jātaka. Ed. Fausböll, London, 1877–1896.
Mahāvaṁsa. Ed. Geiger, Pali Text Soc., London, 1908.
Vibhanga. Ed. Mrs. Rhys Davids, Pali Text Soc., London, 1904.

4. Chinese

Yü Shao-Tsung (ed.). *Hua Fa Yao Lu* (an anthology of Chinese criticism). Shanghai, *ca.* 1930.[2]

[1] *Śilpa Śāstras*.
[2] Not seen by the author.

A CATALOG OF SELECTED

DOVER BOOKS

IN ALL FIELDS OF INTEREST

THE MURDER BOOK OF J.G. REEDER, Edgar Wallace. Eight suspenseful stories by bestselling mystery writer of 20s and 30s. Features the donnish Mr. J.G. Reeder of Public Prosecutor's Office. 128pp. 5⅜ × 8½. (Available in U.S. only)
24374-5 Pa. $3.95

ANNE ORR'S CHARTED DESIGNS, Anne Orr. Best designs by premier needlework designer, all on charts: flowers, borders, birds, children, alphabets, etc. Over 100 charts, 10 in color. Total of 40pp. 8¼ × 11. 23704-4 Pa. $2.50

BASIC CONSTRUCTION TECHNIQUES FOR HOUSES AND SMALL BUILDINGS SIMPLY EXPLAINED, U.S. Bureau of Naval Personnel. Grading, masonry, woodworking, floor and wall framing, roof framing, plastering, tile setting, much more. Over 675 illustrations. 568pp. 6½ × 9¼. 20242-9 Pa. $8.95

MATISSE LINE DRAWINGS AND PRINTS, Henri Matisse. Representative collection of female nudes, faces, still lifes, experimental works, etc., from 1898 to 1948. 50 illustrations. 48pp. 8⅜ × 11¼. 23877-6 Pa. $3.50

HOW TO PLAY THE CHESS OPENINGS, Eugene Znosko-Borovsky. Clear, profound examinations of just what each opening is intended to do and how opponent can counter. Many sample games. 147pp. 5⅜ × 8½. 22795-2 Pa. $2.95

DUPLICATE BRIDGE, Alfred Sheinwold. Clear, thorough, easily followed account: rules, etiquette, scoring, strategy, bidding; Goren's point-count system, Blackwood and Gerber conventions, etc. 158pp. 5⅜ × 8½. 22741-3 Pa. $3.00

SARGENT PORTRAIT DRAWINGS, J.S. Sargent. Collection of 42 portraits reveals technical skill and intuitive eye of noted American portrait painter, John Singer Sargent. 48pp. 8¼ × 11⅛. 24524-1 Pa. $3.50

ENTERTAINING SCIENCE EXPERIMENTS WITH EVERYDAY OBJECTS, Martin Gardner. Over 100 experiments for youngsters. Will amuse, astonish, teach, and entertain. Over 100 illustrations. 127pp. 5⅜ × 8½. 24201-3 Pa. $2.50

TEDDY BEAR PAPER DOLLS IN FULL COLOR: A Family of Four Bears and Their Costumes, Crystal Collins. A family of four Teddy Bear paper dolls and nearly 60 cut-out costumes. Full color, printed one side only. 32pp. 9¼ × 12¼.
24550-0 Pa. $3.50

NEW CALLIGRAPHIC ORNAMENTS AND FLOURISHES, Arthur Baker. Unusual, multi-useable material: arrows, pointing hands, brackets and frames, ovals, swirls, birds, etc. Nearly 700 illustrations. 80pp. 8⅜ × 11¼.
24095-9 Pa. $3.75

DINOSAUR DIORAMAS TO CUT & ASSEMBLE, M. Kalmenoff. Two complete three-dimensional scenes in full color, with 31 cut-out animals and plants. Excellent educational toy for youngsters. Instructions; 2 assembly diagrams. 32pp. 9¼ × 12¼. 24541-1 Pa. $4.50

SILHOUETTES: A PICTORIAL ARCHIVE OF VARIED ILLUSTRATIONS, edited by Carol Belanger Grafton. Over 600 silhouettes from the 18th to 20th centuries. Profiles and full figures of men, women, children, birds, animals, groups and scenes, nature, ships, an alphabet. 144pp. 8⅜ × 11¼. 23781-8 Pa. $5.95

SURREAL STICKERS AND UNREAL STAMPS, William Rowe. 224 haunting, hilarious stamps on gummed, perforated stock, with images of elephants, geisha girls, George Washington, etc. 16pp. one side. 8¼ × 11. 24371-0 Pa. $3.50

GOURMET KITCHEN LABELS, Ed Sibbett, Jr. 112 full-color labels (4 copies each of 28 designs). Fruit, bread, other culinary motifs. Gummed and perforated. 16pp. 8¼ × 11. 24087-8 Pa. $2.95

PATTERNS AND INSTRUCTIONS FOR CARVING AUTHENTIC BIRDS, H.D. Green. Detailed instructions, 27 diagrams, 85 photographs for carving 15 species of birds so life-like, they'll seem ready to fly! 8¼ × 11. 24222-6 Pa. $2.75

FLATLAND, E.A. Abbott. Science-fiction classic explores life of 2-D being in 3-D world. 16 illustrations. 103pp. 5⅜ × 8. 20001-9 Pa. $2.00

DRIED FLOWERS, Sarah Whitlock and Martha Rankin. Concise, clear, practical guide to dehydration, glycerinizing, pressing plant material, and more. Covers use of silica gel. 12 drawings. 32pp. 5⅜ × 8½. 21802-3 Pa. $1.00

EASY-TO-MAKE CANDLES, Gary V. Guy. Learn how easy it is to make all kinds of decorative candles. Step-by-step instructions. 82 illustrations. 48pp. 8¼ × 11. 23881-4 Pa. $2.95

SUPER STICKERS FOR KIDS, Carolyn Bracken. 128 gummed and perforated full-color stickers: GIRL WANTED, KEEP OUT, BORED OF EDUCATION, X-RATED, COMBAT ZONE, many others. 16pp. 8¼ × 11. 24092-4 Pa. $2.50

CUT AND COLOR PAPER MASKS, Michael Grater. Clowns, animals, funny faces...simply color them in, cut them out, and put them together, and you have 9 paper masks to play with and enjoy. 32pp. 8¼ × 11. 23171-2 Pa. $2.50

A CHRISTMAS CAROL: THE ORIGINAL MANUSCRIPT, Charles Dickens. Clear facsimile of Dickens manuscript, on facing pages with final printed text. 8 illustrations by John Leech, 4 in color on covers. 144pp. 8⅜ × 11¼. 20980-6 Pa. $5.95

CARVING SHOREBIRDS, Harry V. Shourds & Anthony Hillman. 16 full-size patterns (all double-page spreads) for 19 North American shorebirds with step-by-step instructions. 72pp. 9¼ × 12¼. 24287-0 Pa. $4.95

THE GENTLE ART OF MATHEMATICS, Dan Pedoe. Mathematical games, probability, the question of infinity, topology, how the laws of algebra work, problems of irrational numbers, and more. 42 figures. 143pp. 5⅜ × 8½. (EBE) 22949-1 Pa. $3.50

READY-TO-USE DOLLHOUSE WALLPAPER, Katzenbach & Warren, Inc. Stripe, 2 floral stripes, 2 allover florals, polka dot; all in full color. 4 sheets (350 sq. in.) of each, enough for average room. 48pp. 8¼ × 11. 23495-9 Pa. $2.95

MINIATURE IRON-ON TRANSFER PATTERNS FOR DOLLHOUSES, DOLLS, AND SMALL PROJECTS, Rita Weiss and Frank Fontana. Over 100 miniature patterns: rugs, bedspreads, quilts, chair seats, etc. In standard dollhouse size. 48pp. 8¼ × 11. 23741-9 Pa. $1.95

THE DINOSAUR COLORING BOOK, Anthony Rao. 45 renderings of dinosaurs, fossil birds, turtles, other creatures of Mesozoic Era. Scientifically accurate. Captions. 48pp. 8¼ × 11. 24022-3 Pa. $2.50

JAPANESE DESIGN MOTIFS, Matsuya Co. Mon, or heraldic designs. Over 4000 typical, beautiful designs: birds, animals, flowers, swords, fans, geometrics; all beautifully stylized. 213pp. 11⅜ × 8¼. 22874-6 Pa. $7.95

THE TALE OF BENJAMIN BUNNY, Beatrix Potter. Peter Rabbit's cousin coaxes him back into Mr. McGregor's garden for a whole new set of adventures. All 27 full-color illustrations. 59pp. 4¼ × 5½. (Available in U.S. only) 21102-9 Pa. $1.75

THE TALE OF PETER RABBIT AND OTHER FAVORITE STORIES BOXED SET, Beatrix Potter. Seven of Beatrix Potter's best-loved tales including Peter Rabbit in a specially designed, durable boxed set. 4¼ × 5½. Total of 447pp. 158 color illustrations. (Available in U.S. only) 23903-9 Pa. $12.25

PRACTICAL MENTAL MAGIC, Theodore Annemann. Nearly 200 astonishing feats of mental magic revealed in step-by-step detail. Complete advice on staging, patter, etc. Illustrated. 320pp. 5⅜ × 8½. 24426-1 Pa. $5.95

CELEBRATED CASES OF JUDGE DEE (DEE GOONG AN), translated by Robert Van Gulik. Authentic 18th-century Chinese detective novel; Dee and associates solve three interlocked cases. Led to van Gulik's own stories with same characters. Extensive introduction. 9 illustrations. 237pp. 5⅜ × 8½. 23337-5 Pa. $4.95

CUT & FOLD EXTRATERRESTRIAL INVADERS THAT FLY, M. Grater. Stage your own lilliputian space battles.By following the step-by-step instructions and explanatory diagrams you can launch 22 full-color fliers into space. 36pp. 8¼ × 11. 24478-4 Pa. $2.95

CUT & ASSEMBLE VICTORIAN HOUSES, Edmund V. Gillon, Jr. Printed in full color on heavy cardboard stock, 4 authentic Victorian houses in H-O scale: Italian-style Villa, Octagon, Second Empire, Stick Style. 48pp. 9¼ × 12¼. 23849-0 Pa. $4.95

BEST SCIENCE FICTION STORIES OF H.G. WELLS, H.G. Wells. Full novel *The Invisible Man,* plus 17 short stories: "The Crystal Egg," "Aepyornis Island," "The Strange Orchid," etc. 303pp. 5⅜ × 8½. (Available in U.S. only) 21531-8 Pa. $4.95

TRADEMARK DESIGNS OF THE WORLD, Yusaku Kamekura. A lavish collection of nearly 700 trademarks, the work of Wright, Loewy, Klee, Binder, hundreds of others. 160pp. 8¾ × 8. (Available in U.S. only) (EJ) 24191-2 Pa. $5.95

THE ARTIST'S AND CRAFTSMAN'S GUIDE TO REDUCING, ENLARGING AND TRANSFERRING DESIGNS, Rita Weiss. Discover, reduce, enlarge, transfer designs from any objects to any craft project. 12pp. plus 16 sheets special graph paper. 8¼ × 11. 24142-4 Pa. $3.50

TREASURY OF JAPANESE DESIGNS AND MOTIFS FOR ARTISTS AND CRAFTSMEN, edited by Carol Belanger Grafton. Indispensable collection of 360 traditional Japanese designs and motifs redrawn in clean, crisp black-and-white, copyright-free illustrations. 96pp. 8¼ × 11. 24435-0 Pa. $3.95

THE RIME OF THE ANCIENT MARINER, Gustave Doré, S.T. Coleridge. Doré's finest work, 34 plates capture moods, subtleties of poem. Full text. 77pp. 9¼ × 12. 22305-1 Pa. $4.95

SONGS OF INNOCENCE, William Blake. The first and most popular of Blake's famous "Illuminated Books," in a facsimile edition reproducing all 31 brightly colored plates. Additional printed text of each poem. 64pp. 5¼ × 7. 22764-2 Pa. $3.50

AN INTRODUCTION TO INFORMATION THEORY, J.R. Pierce. Second (1980) edition of most impressive non-technical account available. Encoding, entropy, noisy channel, related areas, etc. 320pp. 5⅜ × 8½. 24061-4 Pa. $4.95

THE DIVINE PROPORTION: A STUDY IN MATHEMATICAL BEAUTY, H.E. Huntley. "Divine proportion" or "golden ratio" in poetry, Pascal's triangle, philosophy, psychology, music, mathematical figures, etc. Excellent bridge between science and art. 58 figures. 185pp. 5⅜ × 8½. 22254-3 Pa. $3.95

THE DOVER NEW YORK WALKING GUIDE: From the Battery to Wall Street, Mary J. Shapiro. Superb inexpensive guide to historic buildings and locales in lower Manhattan: Trinity Church, Bowling Green, more. Complete Text; maps. 36 illustrations. 48pp. 3⅞ × 9¼. 24225-0 Pa. $2.50

NEW YORK THEN AND NOW, Edward B. Watson, Edmund V. Gillon, Jr. 83 important Manhattan sites: on facing pages early photographs (1875-1925) and 1976 photos by Gillon. 172 illustrations. 171pp. 9¼ × 10. 23361-8 Pa. $9.95

HISTORIC COSTUME IN PICTURES, Braun & Schneider. Over 1450 costumed figures from dawn of civilization to end of 19th century. English captions. 125 plates. 256pp. 8⅜ × 11¼. 23150-X Pa. $7.50

VICTORIAN AND EDWARDIAN FASHION: A Photographic Survey, Alison Gernsheim. First fashion history completely illustrated by contemporary photographs. Full text plus 235 photos, 1840-1914, in which many celebrities appear. 240pp. 6½ × 9¼. 24205-6 Pa. $6.00

CHARTED CHRISTMAS DESIGNS FOR COUNTED CROSS-STITCH AND OTHER NEEDLECRAFTS, Lindberg Press. Charted designs for 45 beautiful needlecraft projects with many yuletide and wintertime motifs. 48pp. 8¼ × 11. (EDNS) 24356-7 Pa. $2.50

101 FOLK DESIGNS FOR COUNTED CROSS-STITCH AND OTHER NEEDLECRAFTS, Carter Houck. 101 authentic charted folk designs in a wide array of lovely representations with many suggestions for effective use. 48pp. 8¼ × 11. 24369-9 Pa. $2.25

FIVE ACRES AND INDEPENDENCE, Maurice G. Kains. Great back-to-the-land classic explains basics of self-sufficient farming. The one book to get. 95 illustrations. 397pp. 5⅜ × 8½. 20974-1 Pa. $5.95

A MODERN HERBAL, Margaret Grieve. Much the fullest, most exact, most useful compilation of herbal material. Gigantic alphabetical encyclopedia, from aconite to zedoary, gives botanical information, medical properties, folklore, economic uses, and much else. Indispensable to serious reader. 161 illustrations. 888pp. 6½ × 9¼. (Available in U.S. only) 22798-7, 22799-5 Pa., Two-vol. set $16.45

DECORATIVE NAPKIN FOLDING FOR BEGINNERS, Lillian Oppenheimer and Natalie Epstein. 22 different napkin folds in the shape of a heart, clown's hat, love knot, etc. 63 drawings. 48pp. 8¼ × 11. 23797-4 Pa. $1.95

DECORATIVE LABELS FOR HOME CANNING, PRESERVING, AND OTHER HOUSEHOLD AND GIFT USES, Theodore Menten. 128 gummed, perforated labels, beautifully printed in 2 colors. 12 versions. Adhere to metal, glass, wood, ceramics. 24pp. 8¼ × 11. 23219-0 Pa. $3.50

EARLY AMERICAN STENCILS ON WALLS AND FURNITURE, Janet Waring. Thorough coverage of 19th-century folk art: techniques, artifacts, surviving specimens. 166 illustrations, 7 in color. 147pp. of text. 7⅞ × 10¾. 21906-2 Pa. $9.95

AMERICAN ANTIQUE WEATHERVANES, A.B. & W.T. Westervelt. Extensively illustrated 1883 catalog exhibiting over 550 copper weathervanes and finials. Excellent primary source by one of the principal manufacturers. 104pp. 6⅛ × 9¼. 24396-6 Pa. $3.95

ART STUDENTS' ANATOMY, Edmond J. Farris. Long favorite in art schools. Basic elements, common positions, actions. Full text, 158 illustrations. 159pp. 5⅜ × 8½. 20744-7 Pa. $3.95

BRIDGMAN'S LIFE DRAWING, George B. Bridgman. More than 500 drawings and text teach you to abstract the body into its major masses. Also specific areas of anatomy. 192pp. 6½ × 9¼. (EA) 22710-3 Pa. $4.50

COMPLETE PRELUDES AND ETUDES FOR SOLO PIANO, Frederic Chopin. All 26 Preludes, all 27 Etudes by greatest composer of piano music. Authoritative Paderewski edition. 224pp. 9 × 12. (Available in U.S. only) 24052-5 Pa. $7.50

PIANO MUSIC 1888-1905, Claude Debussy. Deux Arabesques, Suite Bergamesque, Masques, 1st series of Images, etc. 9 others, in corrected editions. 175pp. 9⅜ × 12¼. 22771-5 Pa. $5.95

TEDDY BEAR IRON-ON TRANSFER PATTERNS, Ted Menten. 80 iron-on transfer patterns of male and female Teddys in a wide variety of activities, poses, sizes. 48pp. 8¼ × 11. 24596-9 Pa. $2.25

A PICTURE HISTORY OF THE BROOKLYN BRIDGE, M.J. Shapiro. Profusely illustrated account of greatest engineering achievement of 19th century. 167 rare photos & engravings recall construction, human drama. Extensive, detailed text. 122pp. 8¼ × 11. 24403-2 Pa. $7.95

NEW YORK IN THE THIRTIES, Berenice Abbott. Noted photographer's fascinating study shows new buildings that have become famous and old sights that have disappeared forever. 97 photographs. 97pp. 11⅜ × 10. 22967-X Pa. $7.50

MATHEMATICAL TABLES AND FORMULAS, Robert D. Carmichael and Edwin R. Smith. Logarithms, sines, tangents, trig functions, powers, roots, reciprocals, exponential and hyperbolic functions, formulas and theorems. 269pp. 5⅜ × 8½. 60111-0 Pa. $4.95

HANDBOOK OF MATHEMATICAL FUNCTIONS WITH FORMULAS, GRAPHS, AND MATHEMATICAL TABLES, edited by Milton Abramowitz and Irene A. Stegun. Vast compendium: 29 sets of tables, some to as high as 20 places. 1,046pp. 8 × 10½. 61272-4 Pa. $19.95

REASON IN ART, George Santayana. Renowned philosopher's provocative, seminal treatment of basis of art in instinct and experience. Volume Four of *The Life of Reason*. 230pp. 5⅜ × 8. 24358-3 Pa. $4.50

LANGUAGE, TRUTH AND LOGIC, Alfred J. Ayer. Famous, clear introduction to Vienna, Cambridge schools of Logical Positivism. Role of philosophy, elimination of metaphysics, nature of analysis, etc. 160pp. 5⅜ × 8½. (USCO) 20010-8 Pa. $2.95

BASIC ELECTRONICS, U.S. Bureau of Naval Personnel. Electron tubes, circuits, antennas, AM, FM, and CW transmission and receiving, etc. 560 illustrations. 567pp. 6½ × 9¼. 21076-6 Pa. $8.95

THE ART DECO STYLE, edited by Theodore Menten. Furniture, jewelry, metalwork, ceramics, fabrics, lighting fixtures, interior decors, exteriors, graphics from pure French sources. Over 400 photographs. 183pp. 8⅜ × 11¼. 22824-X Pa. $7.95

THE FOUR BOOKS OF ARCHITECTURE, Andrea Palladio. 16th-century classic covers classical architectural remains, Renaissance revivals, classical orders, etc. 1738 Ware English edition. 216 plates. 110pp. of text. 9½ × 12¾. 21308-0 Pa. $11.50

THE WIT AND HUMOR OF OSCAR WILDE, edited by Alvin Redman. More than 1000 ripostes, paradoxes, wisecracks: Work is the curse of the drinking classes, I can resist everything except temptations, etc. 258pp. 5⅜ × 8½. 20602-5 Pa. $3.95

THE DEVIL'S DICTIONARY, Ambrose Bierce. Barbed, bitter, brilliant witticisms in the form of a dictionary. Best, most ferocious satire America has produced. 145pp. 5⅜ × 8½. 20487-1 Pa. $2.75

ERTÉ'S FASHION DESIGNS, Erté. 210 black-and-white inventions from *Harper's Bazar*, 1918-32, plus 8pp. full-color covers. Captions. 88pp. 9 × 12. 24203-X Pa. $6.95

ERTÉ GRAPHICS, Erté. Collection of striking color graphics: *Seasons, Alphabet, Numerals, Aces* and *Precious Stones*. 50 plates, including 4 on covers. 48pp. 9⅜ × 12¼. 23580-7 Pa. $6.95

PAPER FOLDING FOR BEGINNERS, William D. Murray and Francis J. Rigney. Clearest book for making origami sail boats, roosters, frogs that move legs, etc. 40 projects. More than 275 illustrations. 94pp. 5⅜ × 8½. 20713-7 Pa. $2.25

ORIGAMI FOR THE ENTHUSIAST, John Montroll. Fish, ostrich, peacock, squirrel, rhinoceros, Pegasus, 19 other intricate subjects. Instructions. Diagrams. 128pp. 9 × 12. 23799-0 Pa. $4.95

CROCHETING NOVELTY POT HOLDERS, edited by Linda Macho. 64 useful, whimsical pot holders feature kitchen themes, animals, flowers, other novelties. Surprisingly easy to crochet. Complete instructions. 48pp. 8¼ × 11. 24296-X Pa. $1.95

CROCHETING DOILIES, edited by Rita Weiss. Irish Crochet, Jewel, Star Wheel, Vanity Fair and more. Also luncheon and console sets, runners and centerpieces. 51 illustrations. 48pp. 8¼ × 11. 23424-X Pa. $2.50